PARADIGMS
IN TRANSITION

PARADIGMS IN TRANSITION

The Methodology of Social Inquiry

RALPH L. ROSNOW

Temple University

New York · Oxford
OXFORD UNIVERSITY PRESS
1981

Copyright © 1981 by Oxford University Press, Inc.

Library of Congress Cataloging in Publication Data

Rosnow, Ralph L
  Paradigms in transition.

  Includes bibliographical references and indexes.
  1. Social psychology—Methodology. I. Title.
HM251.R78   302   80-20045
ISBN 0-19-502876-7
ISBN 0-19-502877-5 (pbk.)

32,701

Printed in the United States of America

To Mimi Rosnow
Bob Lana Bob Rosenthal

Preface

The thesis of this book concerns the reshaping of social psychology as a science that is sensitive to the complexities and contingencies of embedded and potentially changeable structures and processes at all levels of human action. But change cannot be understood except in reference to stability, and therefore it is important to delineate the regularly recurrent patterns of human nature and human societies. This undertaking requires that we cross disciplinary lines as well as venture forth into unchartered territories beyond the realm of a classical paradigm, one that was inspired by a mechanistic world view. I begin by considering the ways in which social psychology has been influenced by this view which, in particular, underlies the method of experimentation. To be sure, not all mechanists are experimentalists (structural-functional theory is an example), nor are all mechanists insensitive to the notion of social change (mechanistic theories of cultural adaptation are an example).

In order to set the stage for this discussion I will reiterate various developments that may be at the finger tips of most committed professionals. These developments have customarily been treated as independent, but I shall try to develop a holistic view by examining them in historical and philosophical perspective from diverse, but convergent, vantage points. In this way we may begin to see why and how they occurred and where they might lead us in the further evolution of our science. For example, I try to show how the work on experimenter bias and demand characteristics was not simply an attack on the failure of experiments or an attempt to rule out artifacts. Examined from the conceptual framework of psychological epistemology, the artifact work was an assault on the principle of objectivity in behavioral science. In revealing weaknesses in the experimental method of behavioral science, this work prepared the way for further assaults which exposed other weak areas, resulting in a kind of domino-effect. It also served to make us thoroughly aware that the interaction between the experimenter and the subject was embedded in a surrounding context of contemporaneous events, which in part defined the nature of the interaction. The value assault which followed this artifact assault made us cognizant of the moral overtones of this interaction and even further aware that we were dealing with embedded processes and not constant entities to be specifically pulled apart and each part then studied in isolation like the parts of a simple machine.

Although these developments have made us super-conscious of the liabilities of the experiment, there are also fundamental assets of the experimental method that need to be clarified and accentuated. Thus I am not an advocate of abandoning the experimental method (which would be like throwing the baby out with the bath water). But I do think it is time that we charted the course of experimentalists in the past, for it is only in this way that we can begin to understand how the experimental method of social psychology came to be enclosed by the fences that mark its conceptual boundaries and prevent entrance to a wider area of application. I use social psychology as the case in point, because the action-oriented aspirations of social psychologists have been so far-reaching and the failure to meet these goals is so much more apparent and frustrating. I trust, however, that the message of the challenge to social psychology will also reach attentive, and perhaps sympathetic, ears in other disciplines as it must in other divisions of psychology, for it poses a threat to the fundamental verities of other areas of human science as well.

Except for allusions to some of Thomas Kuhn's ideas and the recent work of philosophers and methodologists who are noted in passing, I do not discuss modern developments in the history and philosophy of science, although it can be reasonably argued that they are pertinent to the thesis of this book. My reasons for this omission are twofold: first, I believe the work has had relatively little direct impact on the original thinking of most social psychologists in the forefront of the assault on experimentalism and, second, I did not want to cover the same ground as two recent books in this general area. The interested reader will find syntheses of the epistemology, philosophy, and sociology of behavioral and social science in Ian I. Mitroff and Ralph H. Kilmann's *Methodological Approaches to Social Science* (Jossey-Bass, 1978), and Walter B. Weimer's *Notes on the Methodology of Scientific Research* (Erlbaum, 1979). For those interested in the metaphysical problem of recurrence or repetition in nature, a useful introduction of readings would be Charles Landesman's *The Problem of Universals* (Basic Books, 1971). I have also been selective in emphasizing the attacks on social psychology and have highlighted only those that I perceive to have been the most salient in American social psychology. The contagion of unrest sparked by these attacks now permeates the entire field, and in European and American social psychology new avenues of theory and research are beginning to be widely discussed.

The plan of this project took root several years ago when Conrad Smith, a doctoral student in communication who is now on the faculty of the Department of Journalism at Idaho State University, took a tutorial with me on the parallels between social psychology and physics. Our discussions led me to theorize about the limitations of the naturalistic paradigm of social psychology, particularly in the light of the research that I had been doing on artifacts in psychological experimentation. These thoughts evolved and grew over the following years, as events in social psychology unfolded and as correspondence and conversations with colleagues in psychology, including Irwin Altman, Ronald Baenninger, Kenneth Gergen, David Goldstein, Jeffrey Goldstein, Willis Overton, and Paul Secord, and chance meetings with colleagues in other fields, helped me to formulate the theoretical outline of this book. I thank each of these colleagues and also thank the dozens of graduate students in my classes for their constructive arguments and counterarguments and their helpful reactions in general. John Converse, Marianne Jaeger, Allan Kimmel, Susan Kraus, and Sandra Tunis have worked with me in recent years and their assistance in various stages of this project is gratefully acknowledged. I especially want to thank my old friend William McGuire for his comments and suggestions on an earlier draft of this manuscript.

During the period in which this book was completed, in 1980, I was on a study leave from Temple University. I spent part of this time doing research in England and would like to thank Hilde Himmelweit of the London School of Economics and Michael Argyle and Peter Collett of the University of Oxford who made it possible for me to present some of these ideas in seminars. For the courtesy and help that has been extended to me by the staffs of the following libraries, I am grateful: Paley Library of Temple University, Falvey Library of Villanova University, the Memorial Library of Radnor Township, and the Library of the London School of Economics.

Finally, I am indebted to three people in particular who made helpful editorial suggestions, and who have shared their ideas with me for many years. Robert Rosenthal has provided energizing reactions and much-appreciated reinforcement. Robert Lana has been the sounding board that I needed to develop these ideas. Mimi Rosnow has been my constant intellectual and emotional companion. Each in their own ways has been the perfect synthesis of friend and colleague.

Radnor, Penn.   R.L.R.
July 1980

Contents

For there exists a great chasm between those, on one side, who relate everything to a single central vision, one system less or more coherent or articulate, in terms of which they understand, think and feel—a single, universal, organizing principle in terms of which alone all that they are and say has significance—and, on the other side, those who pursue many ends, often unrelated and even contradictory, connected, if at all, only in some *de facto* way, for some psychological or physiological cause, related by no moral or aesthetic principle; these last lead lives, perform acts, and entertain ideas that are centrifugal rather than centripetal, their thought is scattered or diffused, moving on many levels, seizing upon the essence of a vast variety of experiences and objects for what they are in themselves, without, consciously or unconsciously, seeking to fit them into, or exclude them from, any one unchanging, all-embracing, sometimes self-contradictory and incomplete, at times fanatical, unitary inner vision.

—Isaiah Berlin
The Hedgehog and the Fox

PARADIGMS
IN TRANSITION

1 A Paradigm in Perspective

A great part of Western, as of Eastern, philosophy . . . has been a persistent flight from the temporal to the eternal, the quest of an object on which the reason or the imagination might fix itself with the sense of having attained to something that is not merely perduring but immutable.

Arthur O. Lovejoy
The Great Chain of Being

During the formative years that saw the development of social psychology as a distinct science, there was a significant borrowing of ideas from its parent discipline, experimental psychology. These ideas, which had originally been gleaned from natural science by experimental psychology, became the basis of a paradigm or conceptual scheme for social psychology. For a long time this paradigm seemed appropriate and useful in the context of social psychology, providing a perspective and framework for the discovery and comprehension of the "laws" of social behavior. Recently, however, social psychologists have been confronted with doubts about assumptions that had gone unchallenged for decades. This book looks at the past, at the rise of this paradigm, and at its recent decline as a consequence of an effort to relieve social psychology of the influence of experimentalism. It is also about the future, about the possibility that the disillusionment prevalent in social psychology may signal a transitional stage that will inevitably lead to an array of useful paradigms.

In using the term *paradigm*, I refer to Thomas Kuhn's notion of scientific epistemology.[1] Kuhn envisioned scientific

progress as a succession of quiescent periods divided by intense intellectual revolutions in which the prerequisites for
"normal science" were superseded by new paradigms. While
some theorists may argue that social psychology is pre-
paradigmatic, and that the current period of unrest can be dis-
missed as merely one of many chaotic outbursts of a disorga-
nized and floundering field, there is instead abundant evidence that social psychologists subscribe to a coherent
epistemology, dominated by primitive mechanistic assumptions.[2] The principal assumption, which appealed primarily
because it defined social psychology as a science, was that
social phenomena were subject to causal laws in such a way
that under experimental conditions certain determinate results could be expected.[3] By *social psychology* and *social phenomena* I mean to denote standard content areas, as delin-
eated in the writings of social psychologists, as well as the
new synthesizing areas of behavioral and social science.

Kuhn defined a paradigm as consisting of scientific achieve-
ments that were sufficiently unprecedented to attract an enduring group of adherents away from competing modes of activity. Further, he maintained, it was identified by an
open-endedness that was conducive to the unearthing of new
scientific problems; these in turn required resolution by those
scientists whose research was based on the shared achieve-
ments.[4] The argument for psychological mechanism was one
that originally seduced empirically oriented psychologists,
who sought a revolutionary break with the ancient habit of ac-
cepting reason or mere introspection as the supreme authority
to all attainable truth in psychology. The epistemological tool
inspired by this naturalistic paradigm, the method of experimentation, subsequently came to form the basis of the sociopsychological research tradition, which defines those problems that are beyond the scope of empirical inquiry.

I begin by establishing in this chapter logical grounds for
the arguments to be developed in the following chapters.
What is the nature and origin of the mechanical model of
social psychology? What specific events and issues in social
psychology have placed the experimental ideal in jeopardy of
being superseded by new epistemological tools? How may

these events and issues further illuminate our understanding of the limits of inquiry in human science? What outlook is there for the future of social psychology as an empirical discipline? In the discussions that follow, the preliminary considerations of these questions will lay the groundwork for the later detailed discussions of each.

Psychological Mechanism

The source of current instabilities in social psychology may be traced to a fortuitous association of events in the late nineteenth century that led to the rise of experimentalism in psychology.[5] Spurred on by the extraordinary successes in natural science, early psychologists—including Oswald Külpe, Hermann Ebbinghaus, Edward Bradford Titchener, and other students of Wilhelm Wundt—sought to initiate a rational reconstruction of science as a laboratory enterprise, like experimental physics and chemistry.[6] The primary implement of experimental psychology was the hypothetico-deductive method of science, with which universal laws of causal relationships were revealed by testing carefully deduced hypotheses in isolation in a critical experiment to confirm or refute them. Titchener, in his *Prolegomena*, published posthumously, defended his use of the experimental method as follows:

> . . . the universal and peculiar method of science is observation. Since the phenomena to be observed are both complex and elusive, and since human capacity is variously limited, observation is difficult. Science therefore calls in the aid of experiment, which prolongs the time of observation, rules out disturbing and irrelevant phenomena, and allows variation of circumstances. Experiment, which is observation under favorable conditions, is in so far simply an extension of the universal method of science.[7]

Twentieth-century social psychology developed out of this idealization of experimental psychology, inspired by the assumption that the study of human conduct could proceed with the same disinterested curiosity with which physicists studied the refraction of light and chemists studied the properties of substances and elementary forms of matter.[8] If we trace the metaphysical generalization further back into history, however, we find that it was first derived from the mechanical conceptions of Galileo and Newton. To seventeenth and eighteenth-century scientists and philosophers, the mechanical systems hypothesized by Galileo and crystallized by Newton seemed not only an efficient way of reorganizing the clutter of medieval physics, but an impressive argument for the mechanical nature of all reality.[9] Albert Einstein and Leopold Infeld in 1938 wrote about this revolutionary idea in physics that was later seized on as a model of psychological epistemology:

> The great achievements of mechanics in all its branches, its striking success in the development of astronomy, the application of its ideas to problems apparently different and non-mechanical in character, all these things contributed to the belief that it is possible to describe all natural phenomena in terms of simple forces between unalterable objects. Throughout the two centuries following Galileo's time such an endeavor, conscious or unconscious, is apparent in nearly all scientific creation.[10]

Stephen C. Pepper and Morris R. Cohen in philosophy, and Hayne W. Reese and Willis F. Overton in psychology, among others, have discussed how, within the frame of Galileo's and Newton's monumental works, later theorists founded a doctrinal system of principles and tenets that elevated the mechanical analogy to what must have seemed a homologue of all creation.[11] It was argued that the human system, like the physical system of Galileo and Newton, was also determined in its mechanical features, which were immutable and eternal. For psychologists such as Titchener, who sought to establish firm grounds for experimental psychology in the solid surface of physical science, this was the ideal epistemology. The conception of man as a complex piece of machinery was, with a few twists, derived from this basic classical metaphor.

To understand how the mechanical conception was adapted as a basis of sociopsychological epistemology, it might be well to use the simplest possible example, that of a body at rest.[12] To change the position of such a body, it is necessary to exert some influence upon it—to push it, lift it, or let other bodies act upon it. Our intuitive idea is that such a "machine" is operating as if conceptually frozen in space (as opposed to something organic that evolves or develops), and that motion is connected with the acts of pushing, lifting, or pulling (as opposed to some voluntary conscious action).

The social psychology experiment approached human nature and complex social phenomena as if they, too, were independent and self-contained entities essentially frozen in a state of equilibrium, and that "motion" was always first connected with some outside influence, called a stimulus. The machine is a configuration of parts having specified locations; social psychologists who pursued this analogy, consciously or unconsciously, experimented and theorized as if the configuration of psychological parts could also be studied in isolation, fixed somehow in a specifiable homeostatic state. It logically follows that the laws of operation of such a "machine" could, in principle, be expressed in exact quantitative terms, by functional equations that specified the relations among the parts congealed as if they were immutable. It also followed that complete prediction was ultimately possible, inasmuch as the ideal case consisted of a sequence of effects that, like a universe run with clockwork precision, ran according to invariable laws.

In an industrial civilization wedded to the machine, this mechanical model offered a deceivingly simple epistemology for addressing questions of great complexity that had puzzled philosophers since antiquity. In the study of cognitive psychology, whatever was known to be the most complex machine would consistently serve as a metaphor for human cognitive functioning, from a simple engine in the eighteenth century to the analogy of the telephone switchboard and the digital computer in the twentieth century. In the study of learning, psychological theorists embraced a Cartesian mechanical conception that had inspired the reflex model of Pavlov and Hull. In early clinical investigation, physicalistic models were used to further theoretical speculations about the processes of abnormal psychology. In social psychology, the inspiration of the mechanical conception led to an overemphasis on balance or equilibrium, as if all cultural and environmental changes had gone to completion (as opposed to something that is in constant flux).

Assault on Experimentalism

Although these classical assumptions have dominated psychological epistemology for over a century, there is an intellectual revolution at hand in social psychology. Throughout the history of the field as an experimental science, eloquent dissenters had persisted in the background. But in the 1960s and 1970s there was an open assault on the experimental method as the *modus operandi* of social psychology, and it is this siege on experimental social psychology that provides the initial focus of this book. By 1975, the dissent had been churned into a "crisis of confidence" by the agitation of persons talking past each other, with sides being taken for purposes of polemics.[13]

This modern revolution has been manifestly directed against notions of experimental objectivity that became absorbed into the mainstream of social psychology. According to this idealization, behavioral psychologists gathered data that were morally neutral, public, and replicable. They felt that their work was objective and that their search for truth was carried out independent of their personal biases.[14] One aspect of the attack on experimentation has proceeded on the counterassumption that the experiment is credited with properties it does not actually have (objectivity, moral neutrality, and universality).[15] In an attempt to recapture the intellectual excitement and momentum of the revolutionary arguments, I discuss them in the following chapters roughly in the order in which they were advanced.

It is ironic that the initial assault which exposed a basic weakness in the experimental method was launched by experimentally oriented psychologists themselves. Using laboratory methods to distinguish certain artifacts from unadulterated effects in the experimental findings in psychology, empirical questions were addressed to whether such findings could ever be independent of the experimenter's own wishes and expectations. *Artifacts* were interpreted to mean systematic errors or biases, usually attributable to uncontrolled elements of the psychology experiment, but especially to uncontrolled variables resulting from the social interaction between the experimenter and the research subject.[16] On the assumption that the human subject will usually try to discover the purpose of the experiment and then respond accordingly, the expression *demand characteristics of the experiment* was coined by Martin T. Orne to refer to the inadvertent task-orienting cues that governed the subject's perceptions of the experimenter's intent.[17] At the same time, Robert Rosenthal theorized that an experimenter's expectancy or tacit hypothesis may serve as a self-fulfilling prophecy of his subject's responses.[18]

In laying claim to the status of a distinct science, experimental social psychologists had proceeded from an epistemological ideal that failed to take into account the wider implications of studying a conscious human being within a social setting. Following Orne and Rosenthal, however, to the extent that the experimenter communicated unintentionally and differentially with the research subject, or so far as the subject was responding to demand characteristics, the social psychologists had lost some measure of control over the circumstances of their experiments.[19] There was what one critic called a "generalization gap" between the social psychologists' laboratory findings and their scientific and theoretical ideals, as a result of these artifacts that derived from the conduct and context of sociopsychological experimentation.[20]

This generalization gap quickly widened when new arguments were advanced against the supposed moral neutrality of psychological experimentation, which exposed another weak point in the experimental method. Up until World War II the popular conception of science as an endless frontier unbounded by moral constraints remained largely unshaken. Titchener, among others, had talked about the disinterested and impersonal pursuit of scientific knowledge for its own sake.[21] But since Hiroshima, concern about the nature and consequences of scientific research of all kinds had risen steadily.[22] The assault on experimentalism escalated when social psychologists became swept up in this public anxiety during the late 1960s and early 1970s, which intensified as a result of revelations about the hazards of biomedical research. Caught up in this moralistic temper of the times, criticisms were now directed against laboratory manipulations in social psychology on grounds that they exploited powerless subjects with abusive deceptions.[23] A leading case, which was widely reported, was that of Stanley Milgram's laboratory research on obedience to malevolent authority, in which he had subjected participants to an elaborate deception to make them believe that they were giving painful electric shocks to a hapless victim.[24] It was also during this period that American psychologists had become sensitive to the issue of the invasion of privacy, as a result of a barrage of stories of domestic wiretapping by the C.I.A. and F.B.I., and rumors of similar clandestine activities by other agencies. Responding to cries of indignation and demands for reforms within the profession, a committee of the American Psychological Association (APA) adopted a set of guidelines which spelled out the responsibilities of experimenting psychologists to protect the rights of their research subjects. The APA code specifically stipulated that participants had a right to be informed about the nature of the research and to be protected from deception, coercion, and stress.

Social psychology, as all of science, had thus changed from what Gerald Holton has termed an "endless frontier to an ideology of limits"—limits laid down in self-imposed guidelines and federal rules and regulations.[25] In social psychology, however, the crisis of confidence escalated once more when it became apparent that, despite APA's good intentions, the social psychologists were now caught in a double bind. On one hand, if too much information was given to the research participants, their reactions were no longer spontaneous. On the other hand, the rights of privacy and informed consent were jeopardized by the use of deception. Human subjects raised in a post-Watergate society that had learned to distrust authority seemed to search for ulterior motives and alternative explanations even when informed-consent guidelines were scrupulously followed. This posed a moral dilemma, as a result of the conflict between the scientific imperatives of validity and reliability and the societal imperative of informed consent. It now seemed impossible to do certain kinds of research that would have been readily accepted only a few years earlier, thus preventing replication of some classic experiments in order to delineate their area of application in the here and now. Such key experiments in social psychology as Milgram's, it was argued, would inevitably have produced artifacts if they had rigidly adhered to the APA code.

Even as social psychologists were debating this further weakness, amid a period of intensive self-reflection in all fields, the assault continued as a consequence of a growing awareness of epistemological limitations of an action-oriented experimental social psychology. Particularly prominent in this debate was a renewed discussion over the status of social psychology as a science, stimulated by Kenneth J. Gergen's "social psychology as history" notion. Gergen presented afresh the old argument that social facts were essentially unrepeatable just to the extent that they were merely historical.[26] In the case of physics or chemistry the past fact can be directly observed, but in the case of social psychology our principles are established by reasoning upon assumed probabilities. This greater variability of social facts means that the principles assumed by social psychologists are neither definite nor readily verifiable by experimentation.

By the 1970s many leading psychologists who once asserted that laboratory hypotheses should be formulated for their relevance to social problems were expressing disillusionment with an action-oriented approach that seemed to be based almost entirely on a model of inquiry that was oblivious of the dynamic context of human events. William J. McGuire, a prominent experimentalist in the classical tradition, wrote: "Socially relevant hypotheses, no less than theoretically relevant hypotheses, tend to be based on a simple linear process model, a sequential chain of cause and effect which is inadequate to simulate the true complexities of the individual's cognitive system or the social system which we are typically trying to describe."[27] Attempts to deal with artifacts and the value dilemma also appeared to have trivialized the kinds of questions about complex social problems that could ever be answered experimentally in the social psychologist's laboratory.

A Pluralistic Revolution

The final chapters explore the wider implications of these blows against a classical epistemology that has served psychology for over a century, the likelihood of a paradigm shift in social psychology, and the possibilities for a pluralistic intellectual revolution in human science.[28] During an intellectual revolution, Kuhn wrote, there is ordinarily a sense of crisis when scientists, having turned from puzzle solving to worried discussion of fundamentals, produce a radically new paradigm to supersede the authority of the old one. Responding to this siege on the old paradigm, defenders will try to patch it up with "ad hoc fixes," as both logic and nonrational factors are brought to bear in the battle joined by each paradigm's supporters. However, the dispute will ultimately be resolved by a process of conversion and faith on aesthetic grounds, resulting in a transfer of allegiance from one conceptual scheme to another.[29]

As a result of the crisis of experimentalism, many social psychologists who once thought a naturalistic paradigm was ideal for human research now wrestle with its limitations and yearn for a revolution in psychological epistemology. They aspire, as all scientists do, to theoretical generalizations in which the range of knowledge can be applied universally. If complex social phenomena were regular and repeatable, and could be isolated as independent entities without regard to socioecological changes, it should be simple enough to reduce them to elements and compounds and then to adduce laws of behavior from our observations at any point in time. The classical paradigm of psychology was founded on this simple mechanistic premise. However, human affairs and psychological causality are never this simple in actuality, since human nature and complex social phenomena are not mechanical entities but are structural abstractions and relationships that operate in a changeable field. That the mechanical analogy has been tested and found wanting prepares human science for an intellectual revolution, perhaps in the same way that a paradigm shift in physics is associated with the development of relativity theory and the quantum theory.

The word "crisis," from the Greek *krisis*, a division or separation, implies a crucial turning point, as in a disease.[30] The turning point in the crisis of physics came about when a fundamental postulate was thrown into doubt. For centuries, bodies were thought to be specifically determined and exactly located in space and time. The most fundamental postulate of classical mechanics asserted that each physical system could be localized in space at any point in time. In the case of relativity theory, the crisis of physics began when an attempt was made to define the nature of the earth's motion. Within a classical theoretical framework, the answer was to express the earth's motion relative to space, that is, relative to a celestial body such as the sun or relative to other star systems. Newton had asserted that space was absolute, that it acted on objects but objects did not act on space.

However, this fundamental presupposition of Newton's theory disturbed some scientists, who regarded space as merely a property of physical objects, not as something that possessed an independent structure of its own. Einstein and Infeld later wrote: "The psychological subjective feeling of time enables us to order our impressions, to state that one event precedes another. But to connect every instant of time with a number, by the use of a clock, to regard time as a one-dimensional continuum, is already an invention."[31] Could there be any such thing as "motion relative to space"? it was asked, for the classical conception of motion was now unclear. This uncertainty bred further confusion about the concept of absolute simultaneity, the idea that there was meaning in the statement that an extragalactic event was simultaneous with a terrestrial event.[32]

Similar confusion preceded the emergence of the quantum theory. Because scientists were able to observe the tracks of an electron in a cloud chamber, they could be certain of the existence of electrons. But they could not be certain of the "position" or "velocity" of an electron *in situ,* since there were no such tracks within the atom.[33] Problems such as these, which signaled an assault on classical assumptions of Newtonian physics, seemed insurmountable, and for an agonizing number of years the physicists endured a crisis of confidence.

These problems were eventually resolved, of course, by a speculative jump of mathematical imagination, which inevitably led to an array of admissible theories.[34] Einstein's theory of relativity resulted in a radical revision of our notions of the existence of space and time. Space does not possess an independent existence, he asserted, but instead the physical reality of space constitutes a continuous field expressed in terms of the coordinates of space and time. Simultaneity is not an absolute property of two events, but is relative to the observing system. Through Einstein's definition of coordinate time, he had set an example for other leading scientists who subsequently developed quantum mechanics.[35] The crisis of confidence, which led to a reconceptualization of space and time and the formulation of laws for atomic physics, thus resulted in a shifting of perspectives and the emergence of a more analytic physics.[36]

Proceeding on the assumption that in human science, as in physics, there is an array of admissible paradigms each having its own limitations for discovering and comprehending phenomena in a changing world, the final chapters in this book argue for a theoretical liberalization and methodological pluralism in social psychology as a first step. It is evident that the transitional period of instability into which physics entered was a consequence of profound questions that shook the very foundations of the discipline. The answers that resolved these questions resulted in a restatement of the laws, or limitations of the laws, of physics. The crises of social psychology can, I believe, be scrutinized in the same light, for social psychology has also entered into a period of instability as a consequence of questions that shake its own classical foundations. In physics this condition was crucial for preparing the way for the promulgation of abstractions by which it was possible then to redefine the metatheoretical interstices of science. In the same way, the succession of changes in the reality shaped out of developments that strike at the foundations of social psychology may result in an array of admissible paradigms and the emergence of a science of psychology that is more sensitive to the contexts of human events.

2 The Rise of Experimentalism

In principle there is no topic of psychological inquiry which cannot be approached by the experimental method. And experimental psychology is therefore fully within its rights when it claims to be the general psychology of which we propose to treat.

Oswald Külpe
Outlines of Psychology

There is ample evidence that the idea, if not the actual implementation, of the experimental method as a requisite tool of science goes back many centuries. Throughout the thirteenth century and well into the fourteenth century, patterns of rational-empirical verification were articulated as a hypothetical methodology by Robert Grosseteste, Roger Bacon, and others. Grosseteste, at Oxford University, stressed that scientific conclusions were certain *per demonstrationem*, and he argued that it was possible by critical observation to verify his logical assertions about the nature of light, thereby establishing optics as an empirical science.[1]

Grosseteste's hypothetical methodology was crystallized by his student, Roger Bacon, who defended the "very necessity" of experimentation in science and further stressed the importance of quantification as the only means of arriving at "truth without error." In his *Opus maius*, Bacon wrote: "If . . . we are to arrive at certainty without doubt and at truth without error, we must set foundations of knowledge on mathematics, insofar as disposed through it we can attain to certainty in the other sciences, and to truth through the exclusion of error."[2]

Of two ways of acquiring knowledge, by reason and by experimentation (experience, in his words), Bacon theorized that it was only by experimentation that one could actually prove what reason taught. Thus, he asserted, even if a person had never seen a fire, he might be persuaded by a well-reasoned argument that fire burns and injures things and destroys them. But until he had witnessed a demonstration of combustion, he could never accept what he had learned as an indisputable fact, for "reasoning does not suffice, but experience does."[3]

Grosseteste and Bacon apart, the period of the Middle Ages was not conducive to the systematic development of science consistent with the strides of Aristotle's approach in the Golden Age of Greece. First-hand observation was almost completely displaced by the authority of the written word. It was not until the sixteenth and seventeenth centuries, with the revolutionary thinking of Galileo and Newton, that there was a revolt against the word of authority. Francis Bacon, first in line of the English empiricist philosophers of the seventeenth and eighteenth centuries, recalled in a whimsically sardonic anecdote just how far blind acceptance of the written word had superseded empiricism during the Middle Ages:

In the year of our Lord 1432, there arose a grievous quarrel among the brethren over the number of teeth in the mouth of a horse. For 13 days the disputation raged without ceasing. All the ancient books and chronicles were fetched out, and wonderful and ponderous erudition, such as was never before heard of in this region, was made manifest. At the beginning of the 14th day, a youthful friar of goodly bearing asked his learned superiors for permission to add a word, and straightway, to the wonderment of the disputants, whose deep wisdom he sore vexed, he beseeched them to unbend in a manner coarse and unheard-of, and to look in the open mouth of a horse and find answer to their questioning. At this, their dignity being grievously hurt, they waxed exceedingly wroth, and, joining in a mightly uproar, they flew upon him and smote him hip and thigh, and cast him out forthwith. For, said they, surely Satan hath tempted this bold neophyte to declare unholy and unheard-of ways of finding truth contrary to all the teachings of the fathers. After many days more of the grievous strife the dove of peace sat on the assembly, and they as one man, declaring the problem to be an everlasting mystery because of a grievous dearth of historical and theological evidence thereof, ordered the same writ down.[4]

There is a sweep of history from Grosseteste's hypothetical methodology, through Galileo and Newton, who laid a mechanistic foundation for science, to early psychologists who borrowed this framework for psychological epistemology. All the way up to the modern era, through Machian positivism and the unity of science campaign, the sweep continued, until a stylized notion of science had become the vision and idealization for social psychology to emulate.

Galileo, Descartes, Newton

Medieval physics had been a tangle of confusedly interlaced theories and hypotheses that explained everything, but only in a most cumbersome manner. Revolutionary developments occurred during the period from the mid-sixteenth to the mid-seventeenth century which changed all this, by undermining ancient intellectual foundations and replacing them by a foundation of mechanics.[5] At the same time, the possibility of performing scientific experiments was greatly enhanced by the rise of a technological tradition, and new machines and instruments of all kinds were now being designed for civil, scientific, and military purposes.[6]

Galileo Galilei, by virtue not only of his methodology but also his mathematical formulations of experimental results, was a dominant figure in the development of the experimental method of science. His first observations with the help of a telescope, in 1609, provided evidence for the heliocentric theory of Copernicus, which in the seventeenth century was still at odds with Church doctrine on the incorruptibility of the heavens. Galileo's mathematical definition of velocity and acceleration and their dependence in time, his kinematic laws, and his laws concerning the oscillation of the pendulum—these and other brilliant insights inspired the development of mechanics during this period.[7] More important, perhaps, he had set himself against a mere hypothetical methodology, and in a series of dramatic experiments he demonstrated the necessity for critical empirical inquiry in science.

Galileo's writings, in particular his *Dialogo* of 1632 and his *Discorsi* of 1638, were a reservoir of fruitful hypotheses that were tested experimentally by himself and others. He empirically established the mathematical law of falling bodies in his kinematic experiments that involved dropping objects of different weights.[8] Another famous experiment was that done by Pierre Gassendi, the French scientist, in which he tested Galileo's law of inertia, and the classical theorem of relativity,[9] by first throwing a stone upward from the foot of the mast on a swiftly moving ship and then on a stationary ship. In this way, Gassendi demonstrated that in either test the stone would always fall back on exactly the same spot on the ship.[10]

Another turning point, nearly coinciding with Galileo's work, was the rationalist philosophy of René Descartes and his own extremely mechanistic view of nature. In his *Principia philosophia*, published in 1644, he developed the argument that all science could make do with a mechanical or causal explanation of reality, since the entire physical world, he believed, could be likened to a machine and its parts. The complexity inherent in the design and working parts of a machine confront us with wonder as to the nature of its human creator, and similarly, the machinery that constitutes the physical universe demands that we consider the majesty of its Divine creator, God himself, Descartes argued:

> As regards the general cause, it seems clear to me that it can be none other than God himself. He created matter along with motion and rest in the beginning; and now, merely by his ordinary co-operation, he preserves just the quantity of motion and rest in the material world that he put there in the beginning. . . . Consequently it is most reasonable to hold that, from the mere fact that God gave pieces of matter various movements at their first creation, and that he now preserves all this matter in being in the same way as he first created it, he must likewise always preserve in it the same quantity of motion.[11]

In Descartes, we thus have the kernel of an idealization of the explanatory power of a mechanical conception that was to prevail in various stylized forms for centuries.[12] A concrete example of one such form in modern psychology is the notion of the reflex arc, a particular mechanistic doctrine that can be traced to certain Cartesian assertions later embellished by experimental psychologists. Psychologist-historian Richard Lowry has discussed how the reflex model was originally descended from Descartes's acceptance of an ancient arrogation that nonhuman animals do not think.[13] The behavior of an animal was to be understood only in terms of the application of extrinsic forces or external stimuli. In order to frame a scheme by which the animal could behave without the assistance of a rational, sensitive, or nutritive soul, Descartes imagined the animal's nervous system to be filled with "spirits" that on stimulation from external sources mechanically translated the excitation in an action.

This notion could readily account for the observed regularities of stimulus-response relationships, but as Lowry points out, it could not explain why a stimulus sometimes terminated in one action and sometimes in another. The solution to this puzzle was worked out by Ivan Pavlov, with his mechanical notion of conditioned reflexes. By considering the possibility that reflexive connections could, under some conditions, be acquired, Pavlov solved the riddle of changeability, thereby making the reflex model even more convincing. The next stage in the geneology of the model came as a result of Clark Hull's inspiration that a reflex is not an iron-clad connection between one particular stimulus and one particular response. It is a variable connection, Hull asserted. Thus, from Descartes's notion of the behaving organism as "an automaton . . . a machine that moves of itself" to Hull's vision of "a completely self-maintaining robot,"[14] there was a graduated sequence of insights that made the mechanical conception seem more plausible by gradually increasing the explanatory power of the reflex model.

The mechanistic mode of thought and the use of experiments to test ideas marked a turning point in the development of physics as an empirical science. Isaac Newton, born in the year of Galileo's death, extended this empirical tradition by his own remarkable experiments, and the mechanical conception by his theories on the mechanics of motion. Like Descartes and Galileo, Newton believed in the uniformity of nature, a notion that he developed in detail in *Philosophiae naturalis principia mathematica*, published in 1687. Proceeding on the premise that "space is absolute," his laws of motion tied together a number of ideas into a compact mechanical theory that stood unchallenged for over 200 years.

Newton's commitment to the experimental method was no less intense than his predecessor's, and in *Principia* he wrote, "For since the qualities of bodies are only known to us by experiments, we are to hold for universal all such as universally agree with experiments; and such as are not liable to diminution can never be quite taken away. We are certainly not to relinquish the evidence of experiments for the sake of dreams and vain fictions of our own devising; nor are we to recede from the analogy of Nature, which is wont to be simple, and always consonant to itself." [15] Within the frame of this monumental work, it was a natural progression for others to found a doctrinal system of principles and tenets that elevated the mechanical analogy to a homologue of human nature, and experimentalism to the pinnacle of scientific methodology.

Almost immediately, Newton's formulation was embraced by social philosophers who advocated a physicalistic doctrine proclaiming that the vocabulary and theory of mechanics was also adequate to comprehend purposive behaviors. [16] Inspired by such bold extrapolations, it began to be argued that every event in the whole range of natural and human phenomena could be understood by following Newton's principles. Man, after all, was only an example of social engineering or a complex piece of machinery that transmitted and modified force or energy. [17] No less influential was the doctrine of experimentalism: One does not ask *why* a machine works, only *how* it works, and the experiment tells us *exactly* how everything mechanical works.

Locke, Hume, Kant

David Hume's great accomplishment was to show logically that the experimental method could be applied to the study of human relations, thus anticipating the later positivistic revolution led by Comte, Mach, and others. To do this, Hume had to reconstruct the relations of phenomena in natural science, then to explain the nature of the experimental method of reasoning as applied to natural phenomena, and finally to apply this rational reconstruction to human behavior. His *Treatise of Human Nature*, published in 1739–40, was explicitly subtitled *An Attempt to Introduce the Experimental Method of Reasoning into Moral Subjects*.[18]

Proceeding from the methodology of Newton and the empirical philosophy of John Locke, Hume assumed the stance of an antirationalist in adopting a mechanical method to explain how a "determination of the mind" leads us to infer causality.[19] Locke, the seventeenth-century empiricist, had also maintained an avid interest in the relatively new "philosophy of mechanism," and he too may have been consciously endeavoring to construct a Newtonian psychology. "Nothing is in the intellect which is not first in the senses," Locke wrote (his famous dictum of the *tabula rasa*). Even in his political essays there were embryonic fragments of a mechanical conception applied to complex human relations.[20] But Hume went much further than Locke to illustrate the utterly irrational basis of knowledge.

It is intrinsic to human nature to expect that the future will be like the past, Hume asserted. "The mind is determin'd by custom to pass from any cause to its effect, and that upon the appearance of the one, 'tis almost impossible for it not to form an idea of the other."[21] Thus he argued, humans are conditioned by repetitions and by the mechanism of the association of ideas to expect and believe that instances of which they have no experiences will be like those already experienced by them.[22] Hume developed the hypothetical case of a man who was hung from a high tower in a cage of iron. Though the man knows that he is perfectly secure from falling, he trembles from fear nonetheless, as a result of his "custom" of associating mere contiguous events in a causal sequence (the ideas of "fall and descent" and "harm and death").[23] These two relations of contiguity and succession are the sum and substance of all attributed causality, Hume proclaimed, and he enumerated the rules of causal inference.[24,25] For there to be cause and effect in human relations as in nature, the cause and effect must be contiguous in space and time. The cause must precede the effect. There must be a constant union between the cause and effect. The empirical method of adducing these relationships was Newton's, Hume later wrote, for it is by this method alone that we can "discover, at least in some degree, the secret springs and principles by which the human mind is actuated in its operation."[26]

Later in the eighteenth century, Immanuel Kant sought to modify some of Hume's conclusions by advancing the argument that the principle of causality is valid *a priori*. Kant arrived at this position following his earlier adoption of a scientific heterodoxy of ideas. Gradually, however, he became enamored of Newton's methodology, while at the same time he shifted his intellectual emphasis away from scientific speculation to urgent moral concerns (stimulated by Rousseau).[27] By the 1760s, he was expressing doubts that reality could be comprehended solely by cognitive reason, and he began advocating the empiricism of Newton to study the phenomenal world.[28] Like Descartes, Kant reiterated the classical apologia for a purely mechanistic explanation of cosmic evolution, which, he argued, strengthened the belief of the existence of a Creator who was able to imbue matter with properties enabling it to evolve from a chaotic state to a state of order.[29,30]

Positivism

Nineteenth-century physics had systematized the understanding of inorganic nature into mechanics, governed by Newton's laws, and electricity, governed by Maxwell's equations. For the most part, however, the new physics of Maxwell, Planck, and others was virtually ignored by psychologists, who remained transfixed by a classical metaphysics that was already passing into history.[31] There was, to be sure, an effort in physics to bridge Newton's and Maxwell's laws by building a mechanical model of electricity and ether, but this proved unsuccessful due to the dismal failures of numerous experiments to achieve this end.[32] Psychologists, however, still clung to the old vision of a single, universal organizing principle of human nature.

The theoretical structure of electricity began to be widely heralded as a metaphor for complex psychological and social processes, from clinical phenomena to the inferior status of women and "backward races." Thom Verhave has recently mentioned a system developed by G. M. Beard that bore a marked resemblance to earlier eighteenth-century medical systems to explain neurasthenia.[33] According to Beard, whose physicalistic epistemology owed much to the rapidly advancing knowledge about electricity, a neurasthenic was "a dam with a small reservoir behind it, that often runs dry or nearly so through the torrent at the sluiceway . . . ; a battery with small cells and little potential force and which with little internal resistance quickly becomes actual force, and so is an inconsistent battery, evolving a force sometimes weak, sometimes strong, and requiring frequent repairing and refilling."[34] A similar metaphorical and theoretical structure would permeate Freud's early psychoanalytical speculations.

Auguste Comte, also an empirical philosopher, was a prominent figure during this period. Comte, who has been called the "father of social psychology," maintained a persistent advocacy that thinking about human behavior ought to follow the canons of scientific methodology, by which he meant Newton's methodology. The "Newtonian law" was his heuristic means of pointing out the explanatory power of a positivistic doctrine which argued that the experiment provided the most determinate knowledge one could hope for. This was a major tenet of Comte's positivism—that all we can know are logical connections and functional correlations. We cannot penetrate beneath appearances to detect any ontological influences, he argued. The clear proof of the futility of obtaining scientific answers to metaphysical questions, he continued, was that every time someone had tried to say something rational on the subject he had become hopelessly mired in circular definitions. Thus he envisioned a positivistic "social physics" derived from the classical tradition as the most satisfactory paradigm attainable in social science. "No intelligent person today would seek to go any further" than the Newtonian law, he wrote in Cours de Philosophie Positive.[35]

It was in post-Kantian Germany that the Newtonian meta-

phor and Comtian positivism had a profound impact on nineteenth-century psychological thought.[36] Richard Lowry mentions the particular influence on psychology that derived from
the notions of Hermann von Helmholtz, whose principal interest in physical theory lay in its application to organic functioning. Among those early researchers whose ideas were influenced by this conception was Gustav Theodor Fechner,
who began his career as professor of physics at Leipzig and
eventually formulated a program of experimental research in
what he subsequently called psychophysics. In his *Elemente
der Psychophysik*, published in 1860, the Newtonian-
Helmholtzian mechanical conception was taken for granted to
develop the rationale for an "exact science" of the functional
dependency between mind and body. Even in Freud one
found an enthusiastic (but abortive) attempt to construct a
mechanistic psychophysiology. Indeed any homeostatic
model of psychological functioning is mechanistic in nature—
for example, Freud's hydraulic model of motivation or the
equilibrium model that has figured prominently in modern
social psychology.[37]

Development of Experimental Psychology

Perhaps the most important figure in European psychology
during this period was Wilhelm Wundt, often called the
"founder of experimental psychology."[38] The intellectual
background of Wundt's notions about the nature of science
was set by the idealist conceptualization of science, which
took its cue from Kant's philosophy and later developed into
the perception of psychology as an empirical, mathematical,
and experimental science. But Wundt was also sensitive to the
imperative that experimentalism must be tempered by nonexperimental inquiry in psychological science. While this aspect
of his work has been almost totally ignored by American psychologists, for Wundt, psychology included many topics that
could be studied objectively but not experimentally.

Psychological historians have recently made studies of
Wundt's epistemological dualism that proceeded from his
basic distinction between physiological and experimental psy-

chology, on one hand, and ethnopsychology, on the other.[39] Physical causes and effects occupy one closed system that obeys the law of the conservation of energy, while mental forces form another system governed by chains of psychological causes and effects, Wundt argued. His separation of psychology from natural science derived from this crucial difference between physical and psychic causality. He also rejected a narrow definition of social psychology dealing only with questions of modern cultural life, and instead articulated a rationale for what he called Völkerpsychologie, or "folk psychology," having to do with the dynamic interrelationship between human nature and societal changes. Völkerpsychologie, he argued, requires the development of rigorous nonexperimental methods for the scientific study of phenomena that are creations of the social community (for example, language). In contrast to experimental psychology, which uses a transverse method not at all suitable for the study of longitudinal processes, he envisioned Völkerpsychologie to be a psychogenetic science.[40]

Wundt invested an enormous amount of energy in his monumental work on Völkerpsychologie, for he felt that problems of ethno- or cultural psychology provided the context within which to plumb the depths of individual psychology. Indeed, he expected that experimental psychology would soon take a back seat to the nonexperimental study of social psychological problems. The experimental approach, he argued, was singularly unlikely to achieve an understanding of social psychological problems, for the model reduced these complex systems to mere manipulable entities.[41]

Wundt's reservations about experimentalism notwithstanding, it was the later mechanistic portrayal of him that was incorporated into twentieth-century social psychology. The romance with experimental physics and chemistry, and the rejection of an introspective pursuit of pure emotions, shrunk Wundt's dualism to a monistic methodology that left little room for anything but laboratory experimentation and an unrestrained commitment to a radical empiricist philosophy of science.[42] The notion of psychology as an empirical, mathematical, and experimental science was the ideal that prevailed in the views of positivists who stressed the unity of knowledge and the conception of psychology as a natural science.[43] This critical departure from Wundtian dualism occurred even with his first generation of students, including Külpe and Titchener, who were committed to the new philosophy of positivism then associated with Ernst Mach and others.

Oswald Külpe, Wundt's assistant, led the way in rejecting his mentor's acceptance of the notion of psychic causality. Külpe instead argued for a positivistic psychology along the lines of natural science. In his introductory textbook, first published in 1893, Külpe, an ardent experimentalist, developed the theme that psychology, like all sciences, must begin with the "facts of experience," in this case, with the facts of experiencing *corporeal* (not psychical) individuals. "The objects of psychological enquiry would never present the advantages of measurability and unequivocalness, possessed in so high a degree by the objects investigated by natural science, if they could be brought into relation only with the psychical individual," he wrote.[44] He argued further, "There is no topic of psychological inquiry which cannot be approached by the experimental method."[45]

The period from the late-nineteenth century to the middle-twentieth century was one in which the experimental approach became a dogma of psychological ideology. Around 1879 Wundt established his Leipzig laboratory which became famous as a center for those interested in psychology as an empirical science. A few years before, William James—who also admitted a disparity between an experimental and a more human-oriented, or social, psychology—had founded a demonstration laboratory at Harvard University. In 1875, James announced a graduate course in which he made the class take part in experiments that he arranged in a room in the Lawrence Scientific School Building.[46] The historical juxtaposition of these developments, in conjunction with Wundt's publication of the first psychological journal, had the effect of legitimizing psychology as an experimental science in its own right.[47]

By 1892, James's demonstrational laboratory had developed into a genuine experimental laboratory under the direction of

Hugo Münsterberg, another student of Wundt. Experimental laboratories were established in the 1880s by two other students of Wundt, G. Stanley Hall at Johns Hopkins University and J. McKeen Cattell at the University of Pennsylvania. E. C. Sanford of Clark University published a laboratory manual in 1898, and Edward Bradford Titchener wrote his four-volume *Experimental Psychology* covering basic methods (published 1901–1905).[48]

This was also a time in which P. W. Bridgman's *The Logic of Modern Physics* was having an even greater impact on the psychologists than on the physicists, as the psychologists capitulated to objectivism.[49] Bridgman stressed the value of an operational point of view in science. We don't know the meaning of a concept unless we can specify the operations used in applying the concept in any concrete situation, he argued. The experimental psychologists seized on operationalism, both the idea and the word, and insisted that psychological terms and hypotheses, to be scientific, must have unambiguously specifiable operational meanings.

The Ernst Mach Society, begun in Vienna toward the end of the 1920s, was also founded on the fundamental tenet which asserts that definite experiential meaning is a necessary condition of objectively significant discourse. The Vienna Circle, as it was better known, under the leadership of the logical positivists Moritz Schlick and Rudolph Carnap, thus became an influential force in advocating that logic and experience were the sole arbiters of scientific judgment. Science must be cumulative and allow for prediction and quantification, it was argued. Mach, like Hume, in rejecting the metaphysical dualism of the psychological and physical, refused to go beyond what could be learned from experience alone. The Machian positivists contended that there was no reason that psychologists should not aspire to a scientific status comparable to that of physical scientists, as the only difference between the two was the particular point of view of each.

It is no wonder that both scientists and nonscientists alike, swept up by the tide of advance in physics, evidenced a boundless enthusiasm for the scientific method and its use to extend our knowledge of all of nature. Ernest Rutherford, the great British physicist and Nobel laureate who established the theory of radioactivity, wrote in *Nature* in 1923: "Experiment, directed by the disciplined imagination either of an individual, or still better, of a group of individuals of varied mental outlook, is able to achieve results which far transcend the imagination alone of the greatest natural philosopher." [50] Experimental psychologists were also zealous in their admiration for the power of the scientific method. E. G. Boring, an experimentalist and historian of experimental psychology, echoed the positivistic appeal (as well as William James's famous line, "I wished, by treating Psychology *like* a natural science, to help her to become one") when he wrote in 1933: "Historically science is physical science. Psychology, if it is to be a science, must be like physics. . . . The ultimate abandonment of dualism leaves us the physical world as the only reality." [51]

The Modern Era

For a few short years before psychology continued along its positivistic path, the scope and method of science were once more vigorously debated. During the first quarter of the twentieth century, the "structural versus functional controversy" captured the attention of psychological researchers. [52] The structuralist camp adopted as its unit of analysis the animal as a whole, while the functionalist school formed theories concerning the intimate constitution of the ultimate parts of matter. [53] By the end of this period, however, all that remained was the residue of a naturalistic paradigm still very much in the tradition of experimental mechanics.

This positivist advocacy was most clearly visible in the movement called Behaviorism, which entered American psychology in the early 1900s, and entered social psychology in 1924 when F. H. Allport published a textbook based on behaviorist principles. A strict behaviorist account of psychological reality regarded man as a "conscious machine" upon which particular physical phenomena were permitted to act. John B. Watson, in arguing against introspection as unreliable, proposed as an alternative that psychology become objective as were other sciences.[54] He urged the study of only those phenomena that were open to experimental manipulations.[55] Perceived by behaviorists, human personality consisted of an elaborate system of learned responses. Starting with Watson and proceeding through the major neobehaviorisms of Skinner, Hull, Tolman, and Guthrie, the purposiveness of human behavior was perceived as a relic of filtered stimulus patterns and reactions.[56] Ultimately man was a robotlike apparatus, and human development was reducible simply to a mechanistic theory of reality.[57]

Social psychology was touched by all of these events in the rise of experimentalism, and by 1900 a number of sociopsychological experiments had been done on miscellaneous topics such as suggestion, imitation, and social facilitation.[58] However, it is not clear who did the first such experiment. Frances Galton did some preliminary experiments on a social psychological topic in 1886, and other experiments that could be considered social psychological were done by Joseph Jastrow in 1894 and by Josiah Royce in 1895.[59] One experiment that has been frequently mentioned by psychological historians and textbook writers was that done by Norman Triplett, which was published in the *American Journal of Psychology* in 1898.[60] Triplett, who was trained in experimental psychology, was interested in the fact that cyclists reached higher speeds when they were paced or in competition than when they raced alone. Some authors explained this fact as a physical phenomenon due to a vacuum left behind the front cyclist that drew the following rider along with it. Other theories conjectured that staring at the revolving wheels of the leading bicycle produced a hypnotic trance which then enabled a greater mobilization of energy resources. Triplett's notion was based on the concept of "dynamogenesis," which held that the mere sight of others cycling implanted the idea of this action into the cyclist's mind, thus facilitating his action by increasing the energy available to him. Triplett also thought that it should be possible to produce similar effects in the laboratory in order to test his hypothesis. To achieve this, he had boys and girls, ranging in age from 8 to 14, act as contestants in a race where they had to wind a fishing reel as quickly as possible. The results of this experiment revealed that the children performed more quickly on competition trials than when working alone—which could be explained by Triplett's notion but not by the rival theories. It also turned out to be the single most important scientific accomplishment by Triplett, who left academic research to teach pedagogy at Kansas State Normal School.[61]

The further development of social psychology was given enormous impetus by John Dewey's urgent call in 1917 that heralded a turn toward the neglected social view of behavior.[62] Grandiose expectations for social psychology quickly grew, and over the following two decades there began to be a proliferation of experiments in the laboratory and of hypotheses and postulates that emulated those of natural science. Writing in 1926, for example, one writer enumerated a set of lofty physicalistic postulates for social psychology that proceeded from an idealization of "interacting electrons and protons."[63] To be sure, Carl A. Murchison's *Handbook of Social Psychology*, published in 1935, had a distinctly eclectic orientation with only one of the twenty-three chapters being based on experimental findings in the laboratory. (J. F. Dashiell's "Experimental Studies of the Influence of Social Situations on the Behavior of Individual Human Adults"),[64] but by 1954 when the next *Handbook* appeared under the tutelage of Gardner Lindzey it was unmistakably experimental in orientation. By 1931, Gardner Murphy and Lois B. Murphy, in the first edition of their *Experimental Social Psychology*, could list over 800 relevant studies.[65] As early as the mid-1930s, academic social psychology was becoming firmly established as an empirical science, and the model of empirical science was becoming that of experimental psychology.

World War II and Beyond

Dorwin Cartwright, in his review of the more recent history of social psychology, claims that the most important single influence on the development of the field was the impact of World War II.[66] It resulted in a mass migration of social psychologists and graduate students from the campuses to assist in the solution of problems faced by a nation at war. Cartwright writes: "Most importantly, it fundamentally altered social psychologists' views of the field once and for all, as a legitimate field of specialization worthy of public support."[67] Certainly by the end of the war, the experimental approach had become well absorbed into social psychology. German psychologists fleeing Nazi oppression sought refuge in the United States, and social psychology was now almost completely an American enterprise affected by the pragmatic idealism of experimental psychology in this country.

The vision of social psychology as an experimental science now began to be cultivated under the influence of Carl I. Hovland and Kurt Lewin. Beginning after the War, Hovland and his coworkers at Yale University initiated a program of experimental research whose stated aim was to improve our understanding of human psychological processes by studying the effects of communication on attitudes and behavior. An important parallel development in group processes was the career of Lewin, a student of Gestalt psychology, an eminent theoretician and teacher at Stanford, Cornell, the University of Iowa, and the Massachusetts Institute of Technology. Each brought to social psychology his own brand of experimental epistemology.[68]

Hovland, as part of Clark Hull's coterie, emphasized a learning theory approach patterned from S-R psychology.[69] He also stressed rigorous measurement of the dependent variable, hypothetico-deductive reasoning, and the use of elaborate inferential statistics.[70] Lewin and his protegés brought to social psychology an avid interest in clever and elaborate manipulations of the independent variable, the effects of which were examined with simple statistics. In his influential book, *The Principles of Topological Psychology,* he developed the idea of using the non-Euclidean mathematics of topology as a way of modernizing social psychology.[71] But his field theory, in particular his notion of "life space," with its emphasis on the momentary constitution of the situation, did not really go far enough in throwing off the shackles of classical physics.[72] It stressed the topological structure of a situation in a person's life only at that moment, as if all dynamic processes had reached a state of completion.[73] What both Hovland and Lewin inspired in social psychology was a dedication to experimentalism as the driving force behind sociopsychological epistemology. They also were fortunate to number among their students many future leaders of experimental social psychology, who in turn produced the next generation of leading experimentalists.

From this point on, to paraphrase Thomas Kyd, experimental social psychology grew and grew and bore and bore. From 1949 to 1969, the number of experimental investigations appearing in the *Journal of Abnormal and Social Psychology* and its derivative, the *Journal of Personality and Social Psychology* (the most prestigious journal of social psychology), increased from approximately 30 to 87 percent. Conversely, the total percentage of studies that reported social behavior without using an experimental intervention decreased from 63 percent in 1949 to 16 percent in 1959, then down to 8 percent in 1969.[74] *Advances in Experimental Social Psychology* began publication in 1965, a year after *Progress in Experimental Personality Research* first appeared. In quick succession two new social psychology journals with an experimental orientation also appeared—the *Journal of Experimental Social Psychology* and the *Journal of Experimental Research in Personality*, both in 1965. Also in 1965, the Society of Experimental Social Psychology, an elite organization of American social psychologists drawn from psychology and sociology, was inaugurated at the University of Chicago's Social Psychology Laboratory. It followed the then recent organization of the European Association for the Advancement of Experimental Social Psychology.[75]

But not everyone subscribed to a vision of experimental psychology that followed in the footsteps of physics. E. C. Sanford, in his presidential address before the American Psychological Association, warned in 1902 of "a sort of dumb compulsion" on the part of experimenting psychologists "to make our psychological theories accord with physical measurements."[76] The antidote that Sanford prescribed, which he called "essentially anthropomorphic," stood in sharp contrast to the experimental ideal of Külpe and Titchener. And the year that Murphy and Murphy's *Experimental Social Psychology* was published (1931), L. L. Bernard similarly questioned the path social psychology was taking. It led directly from classical physics, and Bernard warned that it placed so much emphasis on the experimental method that it opened social psychology to serious epistemological difficulties.[77] A generation later, his warning was echoed by Gordon W. Allport in the first edition of Lindzey's *Handbook of Social Psychology* (1954) and was then restated by Allport in even stronger terms in the second edition (1968): "Even if the experiment is successfully repeated there is no proof that the discovery has wider validity. It is for this reason that some current investigations seem to end up in elegantly polished triviality—snippets of empiricism, but nothing more."[78]

3 The Artifact Crisis

But when one works with human materials one must reckon with the fact that everyone is a psychologist. How many subjects in a psychological experiment are purely receptive? How many are willing fully to adopt the humble rôle of subject in an investigation of their motives, aims and thoughts? Most, as a matter of fact, are carrying on a train of psychological activity that is rather about the experiment than a part of it by intention of the [experimenter]. "Where did I see that man before?—What is he getting at anyhow?—I wonder if he will ask me about this?—I won't tell him about that.—Could H. have been here for the same test?—How stupid that experimenter looks!—What a loud necktie!—How stupid he must think I am!—When will this be over?"

Saul Rosenzweig
The Experimental Situation as a Psychological Problem

When Galileo wrote in his *Dialogo* that "in natural science conclusions are true and necessary and have nothing to do with human will," he was stating an assumption about the unexcelled power and objectivity of the scientific method, which would be repeated and accepted for centuries.[1] Throughout the formative years of experimental psychology this sentiment was expressed as the dogma of science by leading psychologists, who cooly referred to their human research participants as "reagents."[2] Chemistry too had come under the influence of the classical conception of science, and in chemistry a reagent denoted a substance used in analysis and snythesis to cause reactions to occur. It was as if, in choosing this term for their human participants, the psychologists were manifestly projecting their own envy for the tremendous successes in physics and chemistry. Of course, the nature of chemistry was such that it easily fit the contours of the science of Galileo and Newton; but in psychology the fit was to prove more labored and unnatural. A chemical reagent is a constant entity that, when properly applied, produces an invariant reaction. But the experimental psychologists were working with "test tubes" that were sullied by all of the needs, anxieties, self-deceptions, and intentions of participants who knew very well that their behavior was being scrutinized as part of a scientific investigation.[3]

Throughout this period and all the way up to the middle of the twentieth century, there were early warnings of the artifact assault that was imminent. One precursor of the later investigations was the curious case of Clever Hans.[4] This intriguing investigation, which had nothing directly to do with human subjects or laboratory experiments but instead with a horse who was credited with remarkable powers of reasoning, first drew attention to the possibility that nonhuman as well as human subjects were susceptible to the effects of observation and unconscious suggestion. The power and objectivity of the scientific method of psychology, at least, might be limited by human will.

Clever Hans

Almost since the beginnings of recorded civilization there were reports of "learned animals," but no animal so captured the imagination of the German public and of European psychology as Clever Hans. At the turn of this century, stories circulated widely of the remarkable intellectual feats performed by Hans, who by tapping his hoof according to a code taught to him by his owner, Wilhelm von Osten, was able to answer questions put to him in German. Asked to spell a word, Hans would tap out the letters, aided ostensibly by a code table in front of him. To respond yes to a question he would nod his head up and down; to respond no he would execute a deliberate sideways motion. Asked by an observer how much $^2/_5$ plus $^1/_2$ is, Hans would tap first 9 and then 10 for $^9/_{10}$. He was also said to possess an excellent memory. He knew the value of all the German coins. He knew the entire yearly calendar and could give you the date of any day mentioned. He could tell the time to the minute. If a sentence were pronounced for him only once, he could repeat the entire sentence the following day. He recognized people after having seen them once, even from photographs taken of them in previous years or from pictures that bore but slight resemblance.

In 1904, Oskar Pfungst, a prominent German psychologist, carried out a six-week investigation of Mr. von Osten's horse. Through careful observation and Sherlockian detection, Pfungst succeeded in deducing the processes engaged in by Hans and his questioners that produced this remarkable performance. Hans was, in fact, exceedingly clever, and his cleverness did not depend on the presence of von Osten (who sincerely believed that he had taught Hans to solve arithmetic problems). Almost anyone could put a question to Hans and get the correct response. But there were three conditions that, when manipulated by Pfungst, moderated the horse's cleverness. First, if Hans were fitted with blinders so that he could not see his questioners, his accuracy immediately dropped off. Second, as the distance between Hans and his questioners was increased, his accuracy diminished. From these findings Pfungst concluded that Hans was clever only when he was in visual proximity with his questioners. Third, the horse's accuracy also diminished when the questioner did not know the answer. Thus, it seemed that the horse's cleverness was perhaps due to his "perspicacity" rather than to an "ability to reason."

As it turned out, Hans was responding to very subtle cues given to him by his questioners, not only to intentional cues, but to movements and mannerisms that were made by the questioners unwittingly. Someone would ask Hans a question that required a long tapping response, and the person would then have a tendency to lean forward as though he were settling down for a long wait. Hans responded to the questioner's forward movement, not to the actual question, and kept tapping away with his hoof until the questioner communicated his expectancy that Hans would stop tapping. This the questioner did, for example, by suddenly straightening up in anticipation that Hans was about to reach the correct number of taps. Hans was sensitive to even more subtle cues: the raising of an eyebrow or the dilation of nostrils. Pfungst showed that anyone could start Hans tapping and then stop his tapping by the use of such cues. Of particular interest, however, was that the cues were given to Hans by his questioners unwittingly. Even Pfungst, when he did not consciously mean to cue Hans, cued him nonetheless.

Pfungst's detective work solved not only the mystery of Clever Hans, but provided an object lesson in the way in which behavior was susceptible to unconscious suggestion. If a horse's behavior can be unintentionally affected by an observer's expectations for him, then might the same principle hold for a human research subject who is interacting with an experimenter oriented by his own theoretical expectations and hypotheses? It was to be another fifty years before this problem was addressed and the so-called experimenter expectancy effect was firmly established. In the meantime, there was another important development which, if not directly, at least indirectly contributed to the view that the answer to the question was a definite Yes.

Experimental Artifacts

In 1927, a group of industrial researchers launched a series of field experiments to study the effects of a variety of working conditions on employees' performance in the Hawthorne plant of the Western Electric Company.[5] One variation on these experiments concerned the level of illumination under which the work was performed. It was observed that whenever the lighting was changed, the efficiency of production also changed, but in a peculiar way. No matter whether the illumination was increased or decreased, the workers' productivity steadily increased in efficiency by the same measure. Whatever variation was introduced, the efficiency of production tended to increase. Whether illumination was increased or decreased, or whether hours of work or rest periods were increased or decreased, the productivity always seemed to improve.

Further investigation led the researchers to theorize that the increases were apparently due to the motivations of the workers in response to group pressures to perform well. Most of the volunteers were so strongly motivated, so eager to cooperate, and flattered at having been selected to participate as subjects in the investigation, that virtually all of the experimental manipulations seemed to trigger the workers' best behaviors. The researchers concluded that when special attention is given to a group of workers—for example, by enlisting them in an experiment—the work productivity is likely to rise independent of changes in actual working conditions.

In spite of what seems now to have been an overgeneralization of these findings, the *Hawthorne effect* entered into the vocabulary of psychological researchers.[6] The term became synonymous with placebo effect as a descriptive label of the power of suggestion.[7] The principle of the Hawthorne effect cautioned that the experimenting psychologist be sensitive to unintentional effects of his experimental manipulations that could confound his empirical generalizations and causal inferences.[8] This methodological principle and the Clever Hans incident were duly communicated by generations of academicians to their psychology students, but there was little noticeable effect with respect to the actual impact this knowledge made on how the academicians themselves went about their research. Lip service was paid to the warnings implicit in these case studies, but the business of experimentation went on as usual, without much regard for the potential artifacts due to these uncontrolled variables.

In 1933, a further conceptual advance was made by Saul Rosenzweig, a young psychologist who had just gotten his Ph.D. at Harvard University. Rosenzweig discussed in detail how the experimental situation was a psychological problem in its own right, and he thus anticipated an area of research to be known as the "social psychology of the psychological experiment."[9] Rosenzweig recognized that, ideally, an experimenter might wish that his experimental materials could be differentiated by their component reactions, as would be true in a competent chemistry experiment. But this simply isn't possible in psychology, he wrote: "Because one is obliged to study psychological phenomena in an intact conscious organism that is part and parcel of a social environment, the isolation of factors is difficult from the standpoint of experimental procedure just as it is dangerous from the theoretical standpoint." [10] He speculated that there were three reasons why it was so difficult to isolate psychological factors in an experiment.

One reason had to do with what he called "errors of observational attitude." The chemist must reckon with the heat of his own body, but the experimenting psychologist, Rosenzweig noted, was obliged to deal with a more ephemeral factor, his own attitudes toward his research subjects and their attitudes toward him. A second reason was that there were "errors of motivational attitude." Unlike a chemist who worked with nonhuman materials, when one worked with human materials one had to be aware that everyone is a psychologist. Human subjects, Rosenzweig wrote, carry on a train of psychological activity in which they try to guess the purpose of the experiment and to anticipate how the experimenter will react to their performance. The experimenter is himself often unaware of the insidious ways in which the "motivational attitude" has crept into and influenced the experiment. The third reason, he added, dealt with "errors of personality influence." The warmth or coolness of the experimenter, his utterance of an unguarded word or nod, whether the experimenter is a man or a woman, white or black, Jew or Gentile—these are factors that may influence the reactions and attitudes of the participant.

Rosenzweig also discussed various procedures that might obviate these problems. He especially emphasized the use of "simple deceptions" as a way of coping with the possibility of errors of motivational attitude. But he warned, it may not always be clear on first glance who the "true deceiver" is, the experimenter or the research subject. [11] The *zeitgeist* may not have been propitious for other experimenters to embrace all of his recommendations for coping with experimental artifacts, although forty years later it was.

Experimenter Effects

Since the late 1950s, Robert Rosenthal and his coworkers had been conducting an extensive investigation of the biasing effects of experimenters in psychological studies. (The term "experimenter" was used liberally to denote any investigator who was engaged in an experimental or nonexperimental study of psychological processes.) As a consequence of Rosenthal's research, and of his careful cataloging of all types of experimenter effects, psychologists began to take more notice of the kinds of methodological issues and problems that had been alluded to by Oskar Pfungst, the Hawthorne researchers, and Saul Rosenzweig.

Rosenthal discussed these problems in terms of two classes of biasing effects of experimenters, noninteractive and interactive.[12] The noninteractive class included any type that functioned without influencing the actual response of the human or animal subjects. This type of experimenter effect operated, so to speak, in the mind, in the eye, or in the hand of the psychologist. For example, there are observer effects, in which the researcher unintentionally biases the results because of unconscious recording errors. Rosenthal estimated that about one percent of the scientific observations of psychologists were in error, which is a small percentage if, indeed, his theoretical extrapolation is correct.

Another example of a noninteractive artifact is an interpreter effect, in which the conclusions reached by the experimenter are biased by a particular attitude or theoretical orientation held by him.[13] To illustrate: a study done by John J. Sherwood and Mark Nataupsky gathered questionnaire data from a large number of psychologists who had published comparative studies of the intelligence of blacks and whites.[14] Sherwood and Nataupsky then used seven biographical items (e.g., age, birth order, education) to differentiate among the nature-versus-nurture conclusions drawn by the psychologists. Thus, a psychologist might have concluded that differences between blacks and whites in intelligence were due to innate inferiority of blacks, to environmental circumstances, or he might have asserted that there are no intelligence differences. Sherwood and Nataupsky reported that simply by knowing the biographical background of the psychologists they could make significant predictions of the psychologists' research conclusions.[15]

A third example of a noninteractive effect is intentional bias or fraud, in which there is an outright distortion of research evidence. For a long time these intentional effects were naively believed to be absent in science, because it was thought that an attempt at outright fraud would be too easily detected. The consensus that limits skepticism is what Thomas Kuhn has called "normal science"—it prevails to the extent that research accords with paradigmatic assumptions, such as the classical assumption of the truth and objectivity of the scientific method. However, once such assumptions are challenged effectively, then there is no longer an ideology to dull suspicions of fraud.[16] A case that came to light in the 1970s was that of Cyril Burt, the famous British psychologist whose work on twins had figured prominently in the public debate about racial differences in intelligence.[17] Burt, who was greatly influenced by the eugenics movement in England (along with Ronald Fisher, Francis Galton, and other ardent eugenicists), hypothesized that intelligence is irredeemably determined by heredity, and he produced overwhelming amounts of data to support this conclusion. But it is now thought that Burt fabricated his data, a suspicion that was first voiced when Leon Kamin, a psychologist at Princeton University, became skeptical of Burt's published findings on the basis of Kamin's discovery of internal implausibilities and basic methodological oversights in the data.[18] Extensive investigations undertaken by a London medical correspondent, Oliver Gillie, reported failure to find any evidence that Burt's two chief coauthors had ever existed, and Burt stands accused of having invented these phantom collaborators to lend credibility to his reports.[19] Because Burt is dead, we may never know whether the statistical artifacts in his reported data were due only to his carelessness or, as it has been argued more recently, to a premeditated attempt on his part to engage in outright distortion of research evidence.[20]

The second or interactive class of experimenter effects is a little like Saul Rosenzweig's notion of errors of personality influence—in this case the research participant's behavior is *directly* affected by human elements. For example, Rosenthal discussed how effects of the sex, age, and race of the investigator may produce quite different experimental results: Male experimenters, he observed, tended to act friendlier toward their subjects.[21] There can also be effects of the temperament of the experimenter: Examiners with a warm personality, who administered standardized intelligence tests, tended to obtain higher scores from their subjects than did cooler examiners (who were usually perceived as more threatening).[22]

Situational effects, another kind of interactional artifact, are reminiscent of the Hawthorne effect, in which the environment or circumstances of the experiment lead to spurious results. But sometimes, of course, even the most bizarre circumstances seem to have absolutely no negative effects, which means that it is not always possible to foresee whether biasing effects will result. For example, in one study there were two forms of an intelligence test administered to 171 people. The first form was taken in a quiet room, and the second was taken in a room with seven bells, five buzzers, a 550-watt spotlight, and 90,000-volt rotary-spark gap, a phonograph, two organ pipes of varying pitch, three metal whistles, a 55-pound circular saw mounted on a wooden frame, a photographer taking pictures, and four students doing acrobatics! The events in the second room were choreographed so that sometimes a number of these distractions were operating at the same time, while other times the room was quiet. In terms of outcome, however, the group did as well in the second room as in the first.[23]

Experimenter-Expectancy Bias

By far the most profound and interesting of the interactional artifacts was an experimental variation on what sociologist Robert Merton had termed the "self-fulfilling prophecy."[24] Just as Pfungst had shown that it was the questioner's expectations that became the "reason" for Clever Hans's amazing performance, Rosenthal now showed that the experimenter's hypothesis can also function as a self-fulfilling prophecy of his subjects' performances.[25] Known as experimenter-expectancy bias (and often called "the Rosenthal effect"), the experimenter hypothesizes a certain event and then unintentionally behaves in such a way as to make the prophesied event more likely to occur.

Experimenter-expectancy bias was first alluded to by Rosenthal in his doctoral dissertation, written in 1956.[26] The purpose of this investigation was to demonstrate the psychoanalytical mechanism of projection, defined by Freud as "the ego thrusting forth onto the external world whatever gives rise to pain internally."[27] Rosenthal had three groups of participants (normal college men, normal college women, and hospitalized patients) rate a number of photographs of neutral-looking faces before and after the participants had experienced "success" or "failure" on a bogus IQ test. His supposition was that these different groups would each express their emotional feelings by projecting them onto the faces in the photographs. The success groups, Rosenthal hypothesized, would rate the photos higher in success and the failure groups would rate them higher in failure, as a consequence of their own experiences of success or failure on the bogus test. But contrary to his own expectation, there appeared to be no direct evidence for the occurrence of projection in any of the groups.

Looking again at the data, Rosenthal found that several of his statistical analyses seemed to suggest the presence of a confounding factor that may have influenced his results. He called this factor *unconscious experimenter bias:* It holds that, in certain types of research, there are subtle, important processes of a self-fulfilling nature occurring within the experimenter that can bias the outcome of his research. In asserting this principle, Rosenthal had challenged the classical assumption of the infallibility of the experimenter. It now remained for him to demonstrate this conclusion in a more convincing way.

His extensive findings have been widely reported and vigorously debated,[28] and I shall mention only one such study done by Rosenthal with Reed Lawson.[29] The standard procedure used in these studies was to create two groups of experimenters who differed only in their expectations to communicate a different hypothesis to each group of human subjects. In the study by Rosenthal and Lawson, this information was communicated to the experimenters in a novel way, and the subjects were rats rather than humans. The experimenters in this study were undergraduates at Ohio State University. Part of the requirement in an experimental psychology course was that the students carry out a series of conditioning experiments to introduce them to the field of animal research. The students were told by the instructor that in these conditioning trials they would be using rats who had been continuously inbred to produce successive generations that should perform considerably better or considerably poorer than normal rats. When the students picked up their rats they could see a label on the cages that stated "Skinner box bright" or "Skinner box dull." (Of course, there were no intentional differences between the groups of rats used in the study; the rats were actually labeled bright or dull strictly at random.) Each laboratory team of student experimenters then proceeded to run a series of seven experiments on the rat they had been assigned.

The first experiment, magazine training, consisted of getting the rat to run to the magazine of a Skinner box and eat whenever the feeder was clicked. The second experiment, operant acquisition, involved training the rat to press a bar to get food. Extinction and spontaneous recovery, the third experiment, required the students to record how long it took for the bar-press response to drop out when no food was given to the rat. In the fourth experiment, secondary reinforcement, the rats were again conditioned for food and the response was then partially extinguished; they were then trained to bar-press for a clicking-sound reinforcement instead of for food pellets. The fifth experiment, stimulus discrimination, consisted of training the rats to bar-press only in the presence of a 110-volt light. In the sixth experiment, stimulus generalization, the voltage of the light was decreased from 110 volts to 70 volts to 35 volts and finally to zero, and the animal was taught in each case to bar-press as usual. In the last experiment, chaining of responses, a conditioned loop-pulling response was followed by the light signaling the animal to bar-press in order to receive the food pellet.

The results obtained by Rosenthal and Lawson revealed the subtle influence of their experimenters' expectations on the rats' behaviors. In nearly every case, the rats labeled bright performed better than those labeled dull. Thus there was now firm evidence that the very process of controlled observation could, under certain circumstances, distort the behavior being observed.

While the expectancy effect is neither inexorable nor unquestionably general,[30] a corpus of similar results supporting Rosenthal's contention has since been uncovered in a large number of experimental situations using human research subjects and a wide range of tasks.[31] There has also been speculation and further experimentation on the mediatory processes of the Rosenthal effect, to try to find out exactly how it works. Some evidence has been cited suggesting that the nature of the handling of the rats in the Rosenthal and Lawson experiment may have communicated the experimenter's expectancy, for the experimenters who worked with the "bright" rats appeared to watch over them more carefully (perhaps reinforcing the desired responses by this watchful behavior).[32] In studies done with human subjects it has been reported that the "feeling tone" communicated by the experimenter seemed to act as a reinforcing agent.[33]

It also follows, of course, to ask whether the Rosenthal effect does not raise questions about the objectivity of Rosenthal's own studies. Michael Martin has called this the meta-Rosenthal effect.[34] It means that, since Rosenthal's experiments were also performed by experimenters with their own personal expectations, one cannot know whether these expectations may have affected the results in the direction hypothesized. Rosenthal himself was aware of this confounding effect, and he discussed several control procedures or techniques that could be used to avoid a meta-expectancy effect—although he did not often use them in his own experiments. For example, one might use a totally double-blind design or an expectancy-control design in which different experimenters were given opposing expectations concerning the treatments they would be running and these treatments were then represented in different ways. However, as John Converse recently pointed out, what is to prevent a skeptic from arguing that the results of even this experiment are not to be trusted?[35] The skeptic might argue that there is an infinite regression of experimenter-expectancy effects, and the best we can do is to state our theoretical biases at the outset.

Subject Artifacts

Simultaneous with Rosenthal's initial investigations of experimenter-expectancy bias, an important discovery was made by Martin Orne in his investigations of subject artifacts. Through a series of ingenious demonstration experiments, Orne and his associates established that demand characteristics (the totality of inadvertent cues that conveyed an experimental hypothesis to the subject) could account for spurious findings in the psychological experiment.[36] To the extent that Orne's assertion was true, it would be extraordinarily difficult, if not impossible, to separate subject artifacts due to uncontrolled stimuli from unadulterated effects resulting from the true experimental manipulation.

Orne was primarily interested in the complex nature of hypnosis when he began this program of investigation, and three explanations of hypnosis occurred to him as hypotheses to be tested.[37] What we know as hypnosis might result from (a) the subject's preconceptions of the phenomenon; (b) implicit cues inadvertently given by the hypnotist; or (c) the particular techniques of trance induction. The results of Orne's experiments to assess these alternative hypotheses led him to conclude that what primarily determined the trance manifestations a subject showed on entering hypnosis was the subject's motivation to "act out" the role of a hypnotized person. Both the subject's preconceptions about how a hypnotized person ought to act and the cues communicated by the hypnotist were, Orne concluded, determinants of the subject's expectations concerning how this role was to be enacted.

Empirical support for this interpretation was gathered by

Orne using introductory psychology students at Boston University. In two sections, a demonstration was carried out using several subjects.[38] The demonstration subjects in one section were given the suggestion that upon entering the trance, they would manifest "catalepsy of the dominant hand." The class was then told that catalepsy of the dominant hand was a standard reaction of the hypnotized subject, and the class's attention was called to the fact that the right-handed subject had catalepsy of the right hand and the left-handed subject had catalepsy of the left hand. In the other section the demonstration of hypnosis was carried out, but there was no display of "catalepsy" by the hypnotized subjects.

Volunteers for hypnosis were then asked for within each class and tested in such a way that the experimenter could not tell which lecture they had attended until after the completion of the experiment. Of nine volunteers in the first section, five showed catalepsy of the dominant hand, two showed catalepsy of both hands, and two showed no catalepsy. None of the nine volunteers in the control section showed catalepsy of the dominant hand, but three of them showed catalepsy of both hands. Since catalepsy of the dominant hand, a symptom invented by Orne, was known not to occur spontaneously, its occurrence in the one group but not in the other could be understood as providing confirmatory evidence for Orne's hypothesis that trance behavior is affected by the subject's preconceptions about the hypnotic state. That three of nine volunteers in the control section spontaneously displayed catalepsy of both hands may be explained in terms of the repeated testing for catalepsy, which was also a source of demand characteristics.

In other experiments, Orne observed that research subjects went to remarkable lengths to comply with demand characteristics when they played the good subject role. At one point in his hypnosis research he tried to devise a set of dull, meaningless tasks that nonhypnotized subjects would either refuse to do or would try for only a short time and then abandon. One task consisted of adding hundreds of thousands of two-digit numbers. Five and a half hours after the subjects began, Orne gave up! Even when the subjects were told to tear each

worksheet into a minimum of 32 pieces before going on to the
next, they persisted nonetheless. Orne explained this behavior
as simply the role enactment of subjects who reasoned that no
matter how trivial and inane an experimental task seemed to
them, it surely must have some important scientific purpose
or else they wouldn't have been asked to participate in the
first place. Thus they complied with the demand characteristics of the experiment, Orne concluded, in order to further
the cause of science.[39]

Coping With Artifacts

In the 1960s, further methodological advances were made in
the social psychology of the experiment by many investigators, including Henry Riecken, Milton J. Rosenberg, and Irwin
Silverman, who looked for other reasons to explain the subject's compliance with demand characteristics. Rosenberg and
Silverman, working independently of one another, uncovered
evidence to suggest that the late adolescents who usually
turned up as subjects for psychological experiments responded defensively because of qualms they had about the
normalcy of some aspect of their psychological life. Such subjects often misjudged the powers and analytic interests of the
psychologist to probe the dark recesses of their minds, and
therefore, Rosenberg and Silverman argued, they were motivated to do what they thought the experimenter thought they
should do in order to avoid being judged as deviant in the
clinical sense.[40] Rosenberg termed this state of negative
arousal *evaluation apprehension.*[41]

There was now a constant barrage of studies by these and
many other investigators, which further challenged the objectivity of the psychological experiment. It was about this time
that attentions were riveted firmly to Leon Festinger's formulation of cognitive dissonance, a theory that stimulated an
enormous amount of experimental research and a controversy
as to the validity of its assumptions and assertions.[42,43] Dissonance theory and the artifact assault came into direct conflict
in 1965, when Rosenberg argued that the experimental procedures used by Festinger had produced spurious effects.[44] They

had aroused feelings of evaluation apprehension, Rosenberg
contended, and Festinger's results were not due to his manipulation but to the subjects' motivations to behave in a way that
would not cause them to be evaluated unfavorably. Insofar as
the subjects wanted to avoid being judged as stupid or ill-bred
or greedy or immoral, they had modified their experimental
behavior to project a favorable image, Rosenberg concluded.

During this same period, definitive books on experimenter
and subject bias first appeared: *Experimenter Effects in Behavioral Research* (1966) by Rosenthal; *The Social Nature of Psychological Research* (1967) by Neil Friedman, a former student of Rosenthal's at Harvard; and *Artifact in Behavioral
Research* (1969) edited by Rosenthal and myself. They defined
what is now known about the causes and consequences of artifacts, and in this way provided further tangible evidence of
the wisdom of Saul Rosenzweig's vision thirty years earlier.
They also made abundantly clear the fact that a whole host of
experimenter and subject artifacts threatened the validity and
generalizability of experiments in human psychology. Other
"artifacts" raised by the critics of experimental social psychology included topics such as response sets and styles, the
paper and pencil measures of the dependent variable so often
used in social psychology, interviewer bias, and the ar-
tificiality involved in so much of laboratory research. As a
consequence, the problem of the social psychology of the experiment began to be cited and discussed with regularity in
seminars, textbooks, and technical articles in this and in other
fields.

The stage was set for researchers to seriously contemplate
strategies for coping with artifacts,[45] instead of merely paying
lip service to them (which they had done since the early days
of research on Clever Hans and the Hawthorne effect). However, other events were also transpiring which would make it
more difficult to restructure the experiment and salvage the
old paradigm without making major conceptual alterations.
As a result of ethical objections which began to be made a-
cross a broad front, further procedural and substantive questions were discussed. As far as mistreatment of the human
subject is concerned, not only deception but also stress

(psychological and even physical) of participants was criticized, and other ethical objections were directed against the failure to obtain informed consent and the use of coercion to participate. Illustrative of this value assault is the deception issue and the Milgram experiments which became the focus of an ethics crisis in social psychology.

4 The Ethics Crisis

From a long-range point of view, there is obviously something self-defeating about the use of deception. As we continue to carry out research of this kind, our potential subjects become more and more sophisticated, and we become less and less able to meet the conditions that our experimental procedures require. Moreover, as we continue to carry out research of this kind, our potential subjects become increasingly distrustful of us, and our future relations with them are likely to be undermined. Thus, we are confronted with the anomalous circumstance that the more research we do, the more difficult and questionable it becomes.

Herbert C. Kelman
A Time to Speak

As a further consequence of the artifact crisis, psychologists began to realize that a generalization gap permeated experimental inquiry. It seemed most visible in social psychology, given the very nature of this research.[1] On the assumption that to forewarn subjects was to forearm them (to engage in defensive maneuvers that resulted in artifacts), deception had increasingly become an integral part of experimental research in social psychology. One survey done in the mid-1960s found that 81 percent of conformity studies and 72 percent of studies on cognitive dissonance and balance theory routinely used some form of deception, including giving the research subjects false advance information and false feedback about themselves as well as about instruments, stimuli, tasks and purposes of the experiment.[2] Another survey reported that nearly half of the studies published in 1971 in the *Journal of Person-*

ality and Social Psychology had used deception.[3] Methodological problems in the repeated use of deceptions also were
uncovered—for example, subjects became more guarded in
their reactions once they learned that they had been tricked.[4]

Another way around the artifact problem was to use field
settings and unobtrusive measures of the dependent variable.[5]
But societal concern over eavesdropping and covert observation led to worries about the legality and morality of the use of
unobtrusive measures. In one notorious case, a sociologist had
played the role of a homosexual voyeur in order to observe
hundreds of homosexual encounters in a public washroom in
a city park.[6] In the mid-1960s, when this study was done, the
sociologists had no code of ethics concerning either the need
for informed consent or the inviolability of the subject's right
to privacy.[7]

A few years later, however, privacy as a moral issue had
begun to be recognized quite formally in the law, and many
Americans were expressing concern about threats to the individual's "right to be left alone." Those psychologists who had
turned to field research to avoid the artifact problem were no
less concerned with the moral issue than those who had
turned to laboratory deceptions. The first generation of privacy statutes in psychology grew out of a desire to establish
guidelines to distinguish between right and wrong in the use
of research methods to insure the validity of scientific findings.

Two new dilemmas associated with the conduct of sociopsychological experimentation emerged, one of which is the
subject of Chapter 5—the dilemma that results when research
requiring public support is conducted in the absence of any
guarantee that the resulting knowledge will advance the general benefit of society.[8] The other dilemma, which I now discuss, is that of the balance between the potential scientific
benefits of research against the costs to the rights and welfare
of the human subjects who participate in it. As John M. Darley
has recently stated, there is an ethical imperative in doing
sound research, for if we do not, then "we leave those who are
attempting social change the prey of hucksters who are willing to put forth undocumentable claims based on inadequate

evidence"; but, he added, we must also realize that "subjects have certain substantive rights that cannot be violated regardless of cost-benefit considerations."[9]

The Milgram Experiments

Moral questions were first raised by social psychologist W. Edgar Vinacke, in the 1950s, about the use of deceptions by experimenters.[10] Vinacke, like Saul Rosenzweig before him, understood the scientific benefits inherent in keeping subjects naive by misstating the purpose of the experiment, but he asked whether it was not time to consider the ethical bounds of experimental deceptions. The *zeitgeist* was not yet ready for such an inquiry in 1954, but ten years later Stanley Milgram's behavioral studies of obedience provided the focus that forced psychologists to consider the ethics of the experimental work they were doing. With Milgram's experiments hanging over them, the historical moment was at hand and the second assault on experimentalism began.

The basic design of Milgram's experiments consisted of ordering volunteer subjects, recruited through newspaper advertisements, to act against another individual (a confederate of Milgram's) in increasingly severe fashion.[11] The original experiments were carried out in a laboratory at Yale University, although other experiments were run in an office in Bridgeport, and typical recruits were postal clerks, high school teachers, salesmen, engineers, and laborers. Each subject was assigned the role of teacher and was instructed that he or she could abandon the experiment at any time without losing the small fee promised as compensation. The subject was then seated in front of a "Shock Generator" on which there were switches reading "slight shock" to "danger—severe shock" and indicating increases in voltage from 15 to 450 volts. The teacher's job was to administer shocks to a "learner" (the confederate) every time the learner made a mistake in a simple memory test. The first mistake was punished by a 15-volt shock, the second by a 30-volt shock, and so on up the scale. In actuality, the learner received no shocks at all, but he pretended that he did. He grunted and complained as the "punishment" was increased, and he demanded to be released from his chair at 150 volts. When the punishment reached 285 volts, he gave an agonizing scream and slumped forward. If the subject ever hesitated or protested, the experimenter (Milgram) would say in a calm, authoritative voice, "Please continue" or, "You have no choice, you must go on."

Milgram's experiments dramatically demonstrated the power of a single authoritative voice to elicit obedience. They showed that the antisocial role expectations to which a subject would accede could be violent in appearance. Not a single subject stopped before giving at least 300 volts to the confederate, and about two-thirds of the subjects continued to the end. Obedience to authority did, however, drop off when the teacher and learner were working together in the same room—then only 40 percent of the subjects continued to the end of the experiment. It also dropped off when the experimenter ordered the subject to force the learner to keep his hand on the shockplate.

Milgram interpreted these startlingly high percentages as revealing "the danger to human survival in our make-up." The results, he subsequently argued, raised the possibility "that human nature, or—more specifically—the kind of character produced in American democratic society, cannot be counted on to insulate its citizens from brutality and inhumane treatment at the direction of malevolent authority." [12] He later referred to his research as "the Eichmann experiment," after Adolf Eichmann, the World War II Nazi, who as much as any single individual was responsible for the implementation of the "final solution of the Jewish problem." Hannah Arendt, the political theorist, had written in 1963 that evil did not flourish only because of the insatiable sadism of evil individuals, but instead thrived because of the conventional habits of quite ordinary human beings. [13] Eichmann, she claimed, was quite ordinary. The initial Milgram experiments were done beginning in 1960, while Milgram was at Yale University, before Arendt's book on Eichmann appeared. Milgram later, and again in a 1974 book, argued that his findings were tangible evidence of Arendt's thesis concerning the "banality of evil." The psychological potential to perpetrate horrendous crimes such as those committed by Adolf Eichmann was merely part of our obedient human nature, Milgram contended.

A Value Dilemma

Milgram's research was attacked in 1964 by another psychologist, Diana Baumrind, who raised moral concerns reminiscent of the ethical questions that Vinacke had raised ten years earlier.[14] She argued that Milgram had subjected his participants to psychological risks which, because of artifacts in the research, could have no serious benefit to mankind anyway. She specifically objected to the procedures used by Milgram, which she believed to be harmful because they caused the participants to lose dignity, self-esteem, and trust in rational authority. Baumrind quoted Milgram's own descriptions of the reactions of some of his participants to support her argument:

> I observed a mature and initially poised businessman enter the laboratory smiling and confident. Within 20 minutes he was reduced to a twitching, stuttering wreck, who was rapidly approaching a point of nervous collapse. He constantly pulled on his earlobe, and twisted his hands. At one point he pushed his fist into his forehead and muttered: "Oh God, let's stop it." And yet he continued to respond to every word of the experimenter, and obeyed to the end.[15]
>
> In a large number of cases the degree of tension reached extremes that are rarely seen in sociopsychological studies. Subjects were observed to sweat, tremble, stutter, bite their lips, groan, and dig their fingernails into their flesh. These were characteristic rather than exceptional responses to the experiment.
>
> One sign of tension was the regular occurrence of nervous laughing fits. Fourteen of the 40 subjects showed definite signs of nervous laughter and smiling. The laughter seemed entirely out of place, even bizarre. Full-blown uncontrollable seizures were observed for 3 subjects. On one occasion we observed a seizure so violently convulsive that it was necessary to call a halt to the experiment. . . .[16]

Baumrind asked why Milgram had not terminated the investigation when he saw that it was so stressful to his subjects. She concluded that there could be no rational basis for doing this kind of research, unless the participants were previously informed of the dangers to themselves and effective steps were later assured to restore their state of well being.

Milgram's rejoinder advanced along two fronts. First, he argued, it was not his intention to create stress, and second, the extreme tension induced in some subjects had been unexpected.[17] Before carrying out the research he had asked some professional colleagues for their opinions, and not even these experts had anticipated the behavior that subsequently resulted. He stated that he also thought that the subjects would refuse to follow his orders. Yet in spite of the dramatic appearance of stress, he felt there was no indication of injurious effects to the subjects. Indeed, he had talked with each participant once the study was completed, to try to reduce any tensions that may have arisen as a result of the experiment. The teachers and the learner even had a friendly reconciliation, and the participants were shown that the confederate had not received dangerous electric shocks but had only pretended to receive them. Milgram had then sent questionnaires to the subjects to elicit their reactions after they had read a full report of his investigation. Fewer than one percent of them replied that they regretted having participated in the experiment; 15 percent were neutral or ambivalent; and over 80 percent said they were glad to have participated.

Divergent values can be advocated in the name of morality, as is evident from a comparison of Baumrind's and Milgram's viewpoints. The experimenter in his study was not just any authority, Milgram argued, but one who had told the participant to act harshly and inhumanely toward another person. Baumrind believed the distrust of authority that Milgram seemed to have instilled in his participants to be unethical. But Milgram answered that he "would consider it of the highest value if participation in the experiment could, indeed, inculcate a skepticism of this kind of authority."[18] However, there may be a catch-22 in this disagreement about what is moral or immoral about Milgram's research. Kant, in his development of the categorical imperative, equated morality to intrinsic goodness; yet he opened his work on the *Fundamen-*

tal Principles of the Metaphysics of Morals with the statement, "Nothing can possibly be conceived in the world, or
even out of it, which can be called good without qualification,
except a *good will.*" [19] Milgram deceived his subjects, and that
was "categorically wrong." But it can also be said that
Baumrind's perception of Milgram's experiments was perhaps
colored by her knowledge of his results, while Milgram's perception was colored by his own theoretical set. Is it possible
that had Milgram's results turned out differently, then Baumrind would not have condemned his effort by raising moral
concerns? There is, in fact, some evidence to suggest that perceptions of Milgram's research may be contingent more upon
the outcome of his manipulations than on the particular manipulations per se.[20] Furthermore, had Milgram not deceived
the subjects (that is, if he really had them shock the
"learner"), would the studies then have been more ethically
objectionable?

Artifacts and the Value Dilemma

In her discussion Baumrind raised another issue that seemed
to compound the value dilemma. This had to do with the
ecological validity of Milgram's experimental manipulations—that is, the tenability of the experimental relationships
he reported for valid generalizations beyond the experiment
proper.[21] She argued that the anxiety and passivity generated
by the experimental context of Milgram's manipulation would
certainly have made the participants "more prone to behave in
an obedient, suggestible manner in the laboratory than else-
where."[22] She added:

> The laboratory is not the place to study degree of obedience or
> suggestibility, as a function of a particular experimental condi-
> tion, since the base line for these phenomena as found in the lab-
> oratory is probably much higher than in most other settings.[23]

This theme was subsequently seized on by Martin Orne to
wage his own assault on the ecological validity of Milgram's
experiments. Orne, it will be recalled, found that the experi-

mental context legitimized a wide range of behavioral requests, including some that were antisocial in nature. Some of these were perhaps as intense as the request in Milgram's experiments to administer ostensibly torturous electric shocks. For example, in one experiment done with Frederick J. Evans, Orne had run several conditions to determine whether a hypnotized subject's willingness to carry out an antisocial action was due merely to his motivation to play the good subject role.[24] A number of hypnotized subjects were instructed to engage in seemingly dangerous or antisocial acts. They were told to pick up a 14-inch venomous snake with their bare hands, to extract with their bare hands a dissolving copper-alloy half-penny coin from a glass beaker containing fuming nitric acid, and finally to throw the acid at the experimenter's assistant. In another condition, constituting a control group, subjects who were instructed to pretend they were hypnotized were told to engage in the same acts. Orne and Evans reported that the rates of compliance were almost identical in these groups. Five out of six hypnotized subjects carried out all of the suggested activities, and all six subjects who were simulating hypnosis attempted to comply with the antisocial and injurious activities asked of them. When the subjects were questioned afterwards about their feelings, they told the interviewer that they had assumed some form of safety precautions had been taken during the experiment. (Safety precautions had, of course, been taken by the experimenters, but the participants were not previously told this.)

Based on findings such as these, Orne and Charles H. Holland advanced Baumrind's earlier critique of Milgram's procedures.[25] Orne and Holland argued that the role of the good subject demands that the participant pretend to be naive even when he knows full well that the experimenter is playing tricks on him. Persons responding to a newspaper ad to participate in an experiment were not representative of the general population who would have been skeptical and less obedient to authority outside the laboratory, Orne and Holland maintained. The early experiments were done at Yale University, which automatically led the volunteers to assume that the procedures were scientifically meaningful and ethically acceptable—no Yale scientist would ever ask them to harm anybody, Orne and Holland concluded.

Thus, there were levels within the value dilemma, with each level colored by its own shade of meaning. On one level there was the ethicality question raised by Baumrind, and there was Milgram's reply that values are relative. On another level there was the dilemma involving a difference in interpretation of the significance of the research, particularly its ecological validity. There was also the conflict involved when an experimenter used subjects who might have been responding in accord with their own assumptions, made salient from the time they volunteered and from their first impressions of the experiment (different from the kinds of assumptions they would act on in a real-life experience).

Baumrind further contended that Milgram's experimental situation did not accurately reflect any Nazi situation of real-life experience, his argument as to the validity of Hannah Arendt's "banality of evil" thesis notwithstanding. Adolf Eichmann had no reason to think of his Nazi officers as benignly disposed toward himself or their victims. The victims were viewed by Eichmann as subhuman; he did not feel guilt or conflict because he believed them not worthy of consideration. Baumrind noted from Milgram's own description that it was apparent his participants, quite unlike Eichmann, were deeply concerned about the "learner" and trusted the experimenter implicitly.

Ethical Imperatives

Other social psychologists joined in the discussion of human values in social research.[26] Herbert C. Kelman, in his book *A Time to Speak*, told of his own growing disillusionment, which began during his years in college, with deception experiments. As a result of his early experiences in psychology, including exposure to the studies being done by Kurt Lewin and later Carl Hovland, with whom Kelman collaborated in research on attitude change, the ethics of the experimental manipulation of human behavior concerned him deeply. Particularly disturbing to him was not so much that deception was used, but that it was used without question:

> It has now become standard operating procedure in the social psychologist's laboratory. I sometimes feel that we are training a generation of students who do not know that there is any other way of doing experiments in the field, who feel that deception is as much *de rigueur* as significance at the .05 level. Too often deception is used not as a last resort, but as a matter of course. Our attitude seems to be that if you can deceive, why tell the truth? It is this unquestioning acceptance, this routinization of deception, that really concerns me.[27]

Dramatic cases came to light in biomedical research that resulted in serious damage or even death to human subjects.[28] The matter of deceiving human subjects, whether in medicine or in psychology, had become a public issue. It was discussed in journals, in general magazines and newspapers, and became the topic of congressional hearings and professional conferences.[29] In early experiments on conformity, the confederates had deceived the participants by keeping a straight face while making ridiculous perceptual judgments.[30] The level of deception in experiments had now escalated, and Milgram's manipulation was beginning to look tame in comparison to the bizarre deceptions being used by experimental social psychologists.[31]

Had it been possible to make a blanket indictment of deception, then this matter could have been settled once and for all by resolving to follow one golden rule, Thou Shalt Not Deceive. To adopt a rigid moralistic code would have required that a deception be labeled a deception and that it be banished or ruled out. But most people, psychologists included, prefer to weigh and measure their sins and to judge some to be greater than others.[32] What social psychologist would seriously advocate giving up the study of racial prejudice and discrimination? Yet, if all measures of racial prejudice had to be labeled as such, would it be worth the effort to continue this research? Furthermore, deceptions of a different sort were sanctioned by our value system to monitor a wide range of practices in our society; for example, the use of pseudopatients to monitor the Medicaid system.[33] Would this be an ethical use of deception, or would it constitute a form of entrapment?

In order to clearly define grounds on which to assess whether an experimental procedure was morally right or wrong, it was imperative that a set of value judgments be codified in a formal document.[34] One of the best known codes of research ethics was that advanced at the Nuremberg War Tribunal in 1947.[35] A set of principles provided the criteria for judging the ethicality of medical research conducted by German physicians on civilian prisoners in concentration camps during World War II. Most modern codes of ethics in human research can be understood as deriving from the philosophy of the Nuremberg Code, which stated that voluntary consent of the human subject was required, that the subject must be fully informed of the nature and risks of experimentation, that any such risks should be avoided whenever possible in the design of the experiment, that the subject should be protected against even remote hazards, that the experiment should be conducted only by scientifically qualified persons, that the subject must be at liberty to terminate the experiment at any time, and that the scientist must also be prepared to terminate the experiment if at any time he has probable cause to believe that a continuation is likely to result in injury, disability, or death to the subject.[36]

Proceeding along similar ideological lines, a committee formed by the American Psychological Association (APA) drafted a code of ethics for research with human subjects, which was adopted by APA Council and published in January 1973 in the *American Psychologist.** The basic structure of the APA code consisted of these ten statements:

1. In planning a study the investigator has the personal responsibility to make a careful evaluation of its ethical acceptability, taking into account these Principles for research with human beings. To the extent that this ap-

praisal, weighing scientific and humane values, suggests a deviation from any Principle, the investigator incurs an increasingly serious obligation to seek ethical advice and to observe more stringent safeguards to protect the rights of the human research participant.

2. Responsibility for the establishment and maintenance of acceptable ethical practice in research always remains with the individual investigator. The investigator is also responsible for the ethical treatment of research participants by collaborators, assistants, students and employees, all of whom, however, incur parallel obligations.

3. Ethical practice requires the investigator to inform the participant of all features of the research that reasonably might be expected to influence willingness to participate, and to explain all other aspects of the research about which the participant inquires. Failure to make full disclosures increases the investigator's responsibility to maintain confidentiality, and to protect the welfare and dignity of the research participant.

4. Openness and honesty are essential characteristics of the relationship between investigator and research participant. When the methodological requirements of a study necessitate concealment or deception, the investigator is required to ensure the participant's understanding of the reasons for this action and to restore the quality of the relationship with the investigator.

5. Ethical research practice requires the investigator to respect the individual's freedom to decline to participate in research or to discontinue participation at any time. The obligation to protect this freedom requires special vigilance when the investigator is in a position of power over the participant. The decision to limit this freedom increases the investigator's responsibility to protect the participant's dignity and welfare.

6. Ethically acceptable research begins with the establishment of a clear and fair agreement between the investigator and the research participant that clarifies the responsibilities of each. The investigator has the obligation to honor all promises and commitments included in that agreement.

7. The ethical investigator protects participants from physical and mental discomfort, harm and danger. If the risk of such consequences exists, the investigator is required to inform the participant of that fact, to secure consent before proceeding, and to take all possible measures to minimize distress. A research procedure may not be used if it is likely to cause serious and lasting harm to participants.

8. After the data are collected, ethical practice requires the investigator to provide the participant with a full clarification of the nature of the study and to remove any misconceptions that may have arisen. Where scientific or humane values justify delaying or withholding information, the investigator acquires a special responsibility to assure that there are no damaging consequences for the participant.

9. Where research procedures may result in undesirable consequences for the participant, the investigator has the responsibility to detect and remove or correct these consequences, including, where relevant, long-term aftereffects.

10. Information obtained about the research participant during the course of an investigation is confidential. When the possibility exists that others may obtain access to such information, ethical research practice requires that this possibility, together with the plans for protecting confidentiality, be explained to the participants as part of the procedure for obtaining informed consent.[37]

Informed Consent

The Nuremberg Code apart, formal codes of ethics stressing similar imperatives of research with human participants had already been adopted by several social science organizations, and others soon followed. An international survey done in 1974 found that 24 codes of ethics had been adopted or were under review by national and international professional organizations of social scientists.[38] The philosophy of these codes advocated an open, honest relationship between the scientific investigator and the research participants, with special atten-

tion paid to the necessity for informed, voluntary consent on
the part of the research participants. Very few codes incorporated much in the way of penalties for noncompliance. The
negative sanction for violating the "ten commandments" of
the APA code was censure or expulsion from the Association—by no means considered a severe penalty, for many psychologists engaged in productive, rewarding research careers
without membership in APA.[39]

The absence of legal safeguards notwithstanding,[40] many
psychologists expressed concern that compliance with the letter of the law could introduce artifacts in their experimental
findings. To give a volunteer subject a fair explanation of the
methods to be followed and their purposes, including iden-
tification of any experimental procedures, might lead to
spurious effects that would widen the generalizability gap.
This worst fear of psychologists seemed to be confirmed by
the results of a study reported by Jerome H. Resnick and
Thomas Schwartz.[41] The study took a widely used verbal-conditioning method and administered it under two conditions to
volunteer subjects. The procedures used for one group of subjects was to give them routine information about the experimental task, employing the traditional methods used before
the APA code was enacted. The procedure used for the other
group of subjects was to tell them everything about the experiment, including how they were expected to behave in the
verbal-conditioning task—conforming fully to the new APA
ethical standards. The results of this experiment were unexpected, and somewhat puzzling at first glance. Those subjects
who had been given only routine information behaved in the
usual way in the verbal-conditioning task. However, the fully
informed subjects produced a boomerang effect—instead of
conditioning in the usual way, they conditioned negatively to
the verbal stimuli.

When the subjects in this experiment were asked afterwards
why they behaved the way they did, their responses revealed
a high level of mistrust of the experimenters as a result of having been told so much about how they were expected to behave. One participant who had negatively conditioned told
the experimenters that he simply did not believe them when

they stated the purpose of the task, and that he had studiously avoided allowing himself to be reinforced. Another subject who negatively conditioned confessed that he gave much prior thought as to how he would behave in the experiment, knowing what was going to happen, but he wanted to "play it cool" and to give the experimenters the impression that the reinforcements were not affecting his behavior. Such findings seemed to emphasize the complexity of the ethical dilemma facing psychologists, which was not simply resolved by codifying a set of values in a formal document. Resnick and Schwartz voiced their own suspicion that current laws of learning would be stated differently if all the studies had been carried out under the conditions of informed consent specified by the APA code. There was indeed a conflict of values that confronted the experimenters, who had to weigh professional (and societal) demands against scientific imperatives and then decide which violation constituted the greater wrong.

Events in Washington, D.C., were also leading to a further resurgence of ethical concern, and some psychologists began to talk about a subjects' union and a Bill of Rights for research participants.[42] Several years earlier, Chris Argyris noted that enterprising students at two universities wanted to organize a group that offered informed volunteers to interested experimenters:[43]

> They believe that they can get students to cooperate because they would promise them more money, better de-briefing, and more interest on the part of the researchers (e.g., more complete feedback). When this experience was reported to some psychologists their response was similar to the reactions of business men who have just been told for the first time that their employees were considering the creation of a union. There was some nervous laughter, a comment indicating surprise, then another comment to the effect that every organization has some troublemakers, and finally a prediction that such an activity would never succeed because "the students are too disjointed to unite."[44]

The skeptics were right, of course—the students did not unite to form a "subjects' union"—although what difference that would have made is academic. What was making a difference, however, was the psychologists' old habit of tapping populations of convenience for their subject pools.[45] Years before these events had begun to unfold, Quinn McNemar had cautioned that the traditional practice of carrying out experiments with Psych 1 students was creating a "science of the behavior of sophomores."[46] Now it looked as if a science of informed volunteers was looming on the horizon, and methodologists again began looking for ways to restructure the old paradigm.

The extent to which a useful, comprehensive science of human behavior can be based on the behavior of volunteer subjects is an empirical question, and some pertinent findings were reported by Robert Rosenthal and myself in 1975 which suggested how it might be possible to patch up the experimental method once again.[47] One way was to improve generalizability by enticing more "nonvolunteer subjects" into the sampling pool, while another way was to try to estimate how much bias was actually due to the subjects' volunteer status.[48] But even as we were learning to cope with the dilemma of balancing scientific dictates against the psychological cost of research to the participants, the value assault continued.

Prior Restraint

By the late 1970s, psychologists were becoming accustomed to having review boards peer over their shoulders, and "prior restraint" was becoming the password of the decade. Rumors began circulating about how perfectly innocent experiments had been blocked by institutional review boards. At the same time, substantial criticisms of the performance of review boards were also voiced, and questions were formally raised about their effectiveness in enforcing informed consent guidelines.[49]

In one case an electroshock experiment by social psychologists to test a "suffering-leads-to-liking hypothesis" was roundly attacked when it was disclosed that the voluntary consent of the participants had not been obtained.[50] The university charged with this violation was threatened with a cutoff of all federal funds for research, even though the experiment in question had not been federally funded. Assurances of informed consent and of peer review were explicitly required by the U.S. Government under a provision of the National Health Research Act of 1974, and a university that had any type of federal contract or grant was held accountable to federal guidelines regarding human subjects research.[51]

The artifact assault of the 1960s had made psychologists realize the conditions and consequences of doing experimental research. The value assault of the 1970s made them conscious that they had lost long-established freedoms without even knowing it. Yet even as these events unfolded, the siege continued. The following chapter deals with the most pressing of these new questions which exposed further weaknesses in rigid adherence to a naturalistic paradigm that seemed to foreclose on the temporal orientation.

5 The Relevance Crisis

The existence of experimental methods makes us think we have the means of solving the problems which trouble us; though problem and methods pass one another by.

Ludwig Wittgenstein
Philosophical Investigations

Leading social psychologists in the 1920s were loud in sounding their call for an action-oriented science.[1] Having introduced social psychology as a behavioristic and psychological science, they now looked to that science to contribute to human betterment and a successful and democratic social order. The instrument for producing a corpus of universal facts and laws of social behavior was the method of experimentation.[2] But in the 1960s, doubts surfaced about this ideal of an action-oriented social psychology. The tide of dissent that first stirred up doubts about the objectivity of sociopsychological experimentation was soon followed by a tidal wave of criticisms that swept over the field.

Of concern in this chapter is how social psychology as a model for social action came under attack when it was argued that the method of experimentation was oblivious of how social phenomena were conditioned by developmental, teleological, or historical circumstances. Further, it was maintained that the conceptual scheme of social psychology left no room for free will and individual responsibility, as the naturalistic paradigm proceeded as if human events were mechanically tied together in inexorable chains of causation.[3] What reasonable justification, it was asked, could there be for an action-oriented experimental science that depended on society for research support but turned out little of practical value or benefit to society? The social psychologists who acceded to this view thus found themselves caught in another dilemma requiring a choice about the future direction of their science.

Pure versus Applied Science

After World War I, an important factor in the further development of psychology was the belief by many psychologists that its proper course was the marshalling of facts and principles for their application to social problems.[4] The social ideals of service and efficiency, which had been invigorated by mobilization, now stimulated a postwar demand for "psychotechnology." However, there was also a constant friction in which the leaders of pure psychology and applied psychology engaged in a vigorous defense of their own territorial preserves.[5] The Depression served to heighten this tension, and by the late 1930s both the Society for the Psychological Study of Social Issues and the American Association for Applied Psychology had been formed to represent the social relevancy camp.[6]

On the eve of World War II, psychologists were once again imbued with an attitude of social responsibility. Robert S. Lynd, the sociologist, was one of many prominent scientists who argued that the times demanded that academicians of all disciplines get out of their ivory towers and into the real world. In his book *Knowledge for What?* Lynd called for scientists to formulate hypotheses stressing their relevance to social problems, for he warned: "The scholar-scientist is in acute danger of being caught, in the words of one of Auden's poems, 'Lecturing on navigation while the ship is going down.' "[7] The war years provided an unprecedented opportunity for researchers to pursue the vision of social psychology as an action-oriented science, and a variety of topics was investigated by social psychologists for the government—civilian morale and ways of combatting demoralization, enemy morale and psychological warfare, military administration, international relations, and socio-psychological problems dealing with the wartime economy.[8] The U.S. Army's use of films and other mass communication was studied by Carl I. Hovland and his associates, who resorted to a mode of attack in which experiments on a single variable by controlled variation were conducted.[9] Kurt Lewin and his students amply demonstrated that group dynamics was also subject to rigorous experimental treatment by the use of deliberately created situations under careful controls.[10]

By the early 1960s, however, there was a change in mood, resulting in a resurgence of fundamental research. This development was largely due to the availability of federal support for basic research, and grantsmanship rapidly became a prized skill. Demands for the accountability of scientists who received federal grants were counter-attacked and labeled as anti-intellectual. Many psychologists came to consider social concerns merely as popular fads that were antagonistic to the pure science ideal.

In late 1961, a number of social psychologists were invited to Columbia University to participate in symposia celebrating the opening of the new department of social psychology.[11] Some of those who joined in the discussion were already predicting an eventual nonexperimental trend in social psychology, based on the small undercurrent of criticisms by a few psychologists who did not share the field's enthusiasm for experimental method.[12] Others, however, foresaw the future of social psychology as continuing to be anchored in the physicalist world view that had dominated experimental psychology for nearly a century.[13] The remarks of one participant, William J. McGuire, a leading experimentalist raised in the Hullian tradition, were very much in the latter vein and emphasized the prevailing mood that had resulted in the resurgence of pure research.

McGuire proclaimed that approaching social psychological research from the perspective of application rather than theory was "as inelegant and inefficient as trying to push a piece of cooked spaghetti across the table from the back end."[14] Social psychology, he argued, was already preoccupied with action research even to its own detriment: "We are not here to turn out consumer goods.''[15] What he instead envisioned the field turning out was described with an allegorical story:

> I always ask an undergraduate inquirer why he feels his vocation lies in social psychology. Sometimes the student replies "I think maybe modern psychology has something to offer (or at least could be made to offer something) on the problem of international tensions, or how to reduce them before we all blow ourselves up, and I'd like to work on it." To such I say gently, "My boy, you have a good heart. I admire you. Perhaps you should speak to one of my colleagues here. Or have you thought of the law or the ministry?" But sometimes I get that other kind of student who replies: "I'm interested because I've got a hunch that a person might do some neat things in social psychology by using a little matrix algebra and difference equations." To this one I say, "My boy . . .welcome home." But lest I seem to be insisting that we work only from highly mathematical theories, let me make clear that I feel our social-psychological research should concentrate on hypotheses derived from any kind of basic theory. My objection is only to the selection of hypotheses for their relevancy to social action at the cost of theory relevance.[16]

As night follows day, reactions to the pure science ideal in McGuire's parable were followed by another change in mood. The pendulum once again swung in the 1960s, and there was now a sense of urgency about social concerns as a consequence of the domestic unrest in this nation. Social psychologists expressed discontent with the seemingly benign nature of current experimental questions and argued for a return to Lewin's vision of action research. A turning point in social psychology during this period, resulting in a decisive reinvigoration of action-oriented investigation, was a discussion between McGuire and Kenneth Ring which brought to the fore this strong undercurrent of concern about the state of the science.

Ring versus McGuire

Just as Stanley Milgram's experiments had been the bugbear of the value assault, William McGuire's pure science ideal became the bugbear of action-oriented researchers, who quoted Lewin's rallying cry of "No research without action, no action without research." In his speech at Columbia University in 1961, McGuire had gone on to say:

Some might object that I am calling for science for science's sake, that such an enterprise is perhaps well and good for the social psychologist himself who will feel "the roll, the rise, the carol, the creation." But what does it offer to the rest, to the outside world, that justifies the capital expenditure required? I say it offers the rest a joy I can hardly express. It offers him the contemplation of the work itself, like the unraveling of the hemoglobin molecule or Kronecker's solution of the general equation of the fifth degree, the contemplation of the work itself shakes us like a banner. The observer doesn't ask "What is it for?" or "What good is it?" but contemplates it with a feeling of elation and a reverence, with a pride in his humanity, no way else attainable than in knowing he shares his manhood with those who created such excellence. Then he stands up peerless.[17]

Writing in the *Journal of Experimental Social Psychology* in 1967, Kenneth Ring took strong issue with McGuire's lofty vision of social psychology.[18] Ring objected to what he perceived as a growing cleavage between pure science and action-oriented science. The hard-headed values embodied in McGuire's conception of social psychology reflected one Lewinian credo ("Nothing is so practical as a good theory"), but his philosophy could not have been more at odds with Lewin's almost heroic vision of a humanistic, action-oriented social psychology.[19] In calling for an end to the ideal of the detached, scientifically-oriented psychologist, Ring instead argued for the progressivism of a positivistic faith which believes that knowledge is cumulative and leads to a better moral order.[20] The joke of "fun and games" has begun to wear thin, Ring argued, and students are not as likely as their mentors to be impressed with the social psychologist's feats of ingenuity:

They begin to wonder, with increasing impatience, whether social psychology is mainly a matter of style, not substance. What is the perceptive student to think, finally, of a field where the

most renowned researchers apparently get their kicks from prac-
ticing sometimes unnecessary and frankly crass deceptions on
their unsuspecting subjects?[21]

McGuire replied to this argument, answering that for him
the whole idea of the method of experimentation had begun to
wear thin.[22] He drew attention to the artifact assault that was
gathering momentum, and to the ethics assault that was imminent. What is needed, McGuire argued, is a reorientation in
social psychology, especially in the use of the natural environment as a field in which to test theoretical deductions.

The sober reflection and sense of high purpose called for by
Ring and McGuire slowly began to have an impact on the
thinking of social psychologists. Some followed McGuire's advice and turned to the natural environment as a field of study
to test their hypotheses. Others were more persuaded by
Ring's call for a return to the Lewinian ideal in which social
psychologists asked themselves before initiating research
whether the project to be undertaken really represented a
problem of human significance and not merely someone's pet
eccentricity. Soon there was a proliferation of new action-
oriented and applied sociopsychological journals on environmental psychology, gender effects, aggression, and so on. A
scant four years after Ring's article had appeared, psychologists were calling this "the age of relevance in social psychology."

Not all social psychologists were happy with this new turn
of events in the direction of social relevance. Irwin Silverman
questioned "the relevance of relevance."[23] Textbooks in social
psychology, as in other fields, were loaded with topics of
enormous potential social relevance (affiliation, aggression, attitudes, social power), yet little technological data had actually been provided by the social psychologists that was relevant to social ills, Silverman maintained. "It must be that our
data are not generalizable to the objects of our studies in their
natural ongoing states. This is a basic inadequacy of methodology rather than direction, and it will not be resolved by pon-
tifical edicts from any source about what to study and where."
Silverman concluded that the proliferation of "pseudo-

knowledge" within psychology could be attributed to the discipline's "naive acquiescence to externally imposed mandates" and to a "persistent, slavish obsession to fit the study of behavior into existent models of other experimental sciences."[24]

Social Psychology as History

During the first quarter of the twentieth century, when the structure-versus-function controversy was raging, psychologists had vigorously debated the scope and method of science. In the mid-1970s, an article written by Kenneth J. Gergen provided the intellectual impetus for social psychologists to return to this old question about the scientific status of their discipline.[25] Gergen entered the fray in 1973, when he asserted that the scientific model, as he understood it, simply did not apply to social psychology. He argued that the success of the natural sciences in establishing universal laws was due to the fact that events in the world of nature were stable and could be reproduced in anyone's laboratory, but in social psychology the most profound events were capricious and largely nonrepeatable.[26] He noted the example of Stanley Milgram's experiments on obedience to malevolent authority, and contended that they would be generalizable only to the extent that contemporary attitudes toward authority were consistent with those reflected in these studies. In the same way, Gergen went on, cognitive dissonance theory depends on the assumption that persons cannot tolerate contradictory beliefs, but the basis of this assumption is environmentally and historically (not genetically) given. Similar limitations can be shown to apply in the case of an elementary theory of reinforcement, for reinforcers, he argued, do not remain stable across time. Thus, social psychological facts cannot accumulate or grow in the usual scientific sense, because they do not transcend historical boundaries.[27]

Gergen also theorized that teaching people about psychology made them resistant to certain psychological influences, thereby invalidating the underlying principles of what they were taught. This so-called enlightenment effect was first discussed by Gordon W. Allport and Leo Postman in the 1940s in their studies of the psychology of rumor: "It sometimes happens that as soon as a man understands what makes him behave in a certain way, he proceeds to behave differently. . . . And so it is that a person who is 'rumor wise,' who understands that he is likely under conditions of importance and ambiguity to believe and spread rumors, is for that very reason less likely to do so!"[28] Gergen argued, however, that it is impossible to generate *any* universal laws in social psychology, inasmuch as human events always occur within a highly complex network of contingencies that remains in constant flux.

For these reasons, he concluded, social psychology is an historical as opposed to a scientific enterprise. Sociopsychological facts are like still-photographs of some fleeting event that passes into history at the very moment the picture is taken—this was Gergen's social-psychology-as-history argument. Thus, it makes no sense for social psychologists to engage in fundamental research for the purpose of generating transhistorical principles, for they are bound to be frustrated in this quest, if Gergen's argument is correct. There are simply no reasonable grounds for defending the position that pure research in social psychology can ever contribute to basic and enduring knowledge, he asserted.

The swell of controversy generated by Gergen's extreme skepticism (reminiscent perhaps of classical arguments of subjective idealism) led to another intensive colloquy of arguments among social psychologists, already in the throes of the artifact and the ethics assaults.[29] His basic assertion of the immutability of physical entities in natural science seemed a throwback to seventeenth-century theological simplifications of the superiority of immutability to change, which Galileo had challenged with a vengeance in his *Dialogo*. To many psychologists, Gergen seemed simply to have misunderstood the nature of natural science, which was not as rigidly defined as he had conceived it; his argument was based on a false premise, it was maintained. But whatever logical lapses may have weakened or invalidated his presuppositions, his assertion that all things human are subject to historical change was an inescapable conclusion that could not be easily refuted.[30]

Forty years earlier, Morris R. Cohen had also discussed the historical character of social facts. He recognized both the historic and the teleologic aspect of social life, in which, he pointed out, "we see an interaction and a mutual dependence between the descriptive and the normative, between the actual historic cause and the ideal demands of a given system."[31] But he refuted the argument which insists that natural science deals only with abstract aspects of phenomena that can be indefinitely repeated while social science deals only with events that are unique—Cohen pointed to geology as both a historic and a natural science. Social facts also depend upon historical continuity, on some reference to the past, he noted, although it would be hasty and false to conclude that the full nature of social phenomena can be found entirely in their history.

Yin and Yang of Progress

There is a well-known principle of attitude which asserts that thinking polarizes attitudes and beliefs. In his reply to Kenneth Ring, William McGuire had already begun to doubt his earlier dependence on experimentalism, and in 1973 McGuire wrote another article making it clear that his persistent critical thinking about the experimental method had produced a still further polarization in his beliefs.[32] He once more recalled the whole litany of complaints against the method of experimentation, which had originally shaken his confidence. The research on artifacts had convinced him that laboratory experiments were full of experimenter bias, demand characteristics, and evaluation apprehension. As a result of social concern, an increased generalization gap had developed due to ethical constraints that produced sampling biases. On an epistemological level, he argued, the switch from theory relevance to social relevance was merely a superificial cosmetic change that masked rather than corrected the basic problems of experimentalism. We begin with hypotheses that are self-evident and which we will not reject whatever is the experimental outcome, he wrote. We don't use experiments to test our hypotheses, but to demonstrate their obvious truth. What the experiment ultimately tests is "whether the experimenter is a sufficiently ingenious stage manager to produce in the laboratory conditions which demonstrate that an obviously true hypothesis is correct."[33] Moreover, he argued, the emerging use of field experiments—contrary to his earlier expectations—did not solve these problems, for they were inherent in the paradigm of social psychology.

Calling for a new paradigm, McGuire described some steps that might be taken to improve the state of social psychology. We can begin, he argued, by emphasizing the full range of alternatives in generating creative theories and hypotheses, not simply an idealized hypothetico-deductive process of generating and testing hypotheses. We can also begin to think "complexly" in terms of nets of causally interrelated factors, feedback loops, and bidirectional causation, as opposed to a simple linear-process model. We can observe people, not merely sanitized experimental data in the form of computer printouts. We can venture backwards in time by using archival data, but also forwards in time by repeating surveys into the future. We can cultivate new sources of data, and our students can be taught how to cope with the "dirty data" of the real world. We can pursue the more solitary and reflective intellectual activity of integrating isolated findings instead of churning out one little experiment after another and never seeing the work as a whole. In sum, he argued, let us not worship consistency or simplicity if it blinds us to a very fundamental paradox—"the opposite of a great truth is also true." In pursuing a methodological and theoretical pluralism that urges what seem to be opposite courses of action at the same time, we may ever more quickly discover a new paradigm to replace our obsolete one.

Current State

At this writing the siege on experimentalism continues, while at the same time there seems to be an increasing interest in applied or technological questions of all kinds. Reflecting this eclecticism, which may be a prelude to the new paradigm called for by McGuire and others, innovative journals and series have been created to develop formats that are receptive to reports and discussions outside the mainstream of social psychology as it was traditionally defined. The repudiation of experimentalism,[34] along with the realization that social phenomena are less repeatable than those of natural science, has sensitized many social psychologists to the need for the sort of historic and teleologic outlook on social life that was discussed by Morris R. Cohen in 1931. For Cohen, as well as for many modern social psychologists, the distinctive subject-matter of social psychology is culture,[35] and the substances of culture—language, tools, moral habits, enculturated dispositions, etc.—are conditioned by transitory events. The following chapters attempt to put these notions into theoretical perspective by drawing upon other epistemological ideas that have also led to a reconceptualization of the picture of reality.

6 Limits of a Paradigm

> Closed theories . . . take shape, as if from a crystal nucleus, out of individual queries raised about experience, and which eventually, once the complete crystal has developed, again detach themselves from experience as purely intellectual structures that nonetheless forever illuminate the world for us.
>
> Werner Heisenberg
> *Across the Frontiers*

The dust has not yet settled from the assaults on the method of experimentation; indeed its viability remains seriously in question. Can the experiment, as the method of choice in social psychology, fulfill whatever expectations of success were nurtured by the considerable successes resulting from its use in physics and chemistry? Instead of illuminating complex social processes, it is now argued that the simplification inherent in the experimental method focuses on isolated, arbitrary, and trivial aspects of the phenomena under study. Even when the experiment does reveal basic processes, artifacts may render the findings of little value for understanding real-world phenomena. Concerns such as these are expressed not only in social psychology but throughout experimental psychology, leaving many to conclude that the experimental method, now one hundred years old, is truly an antique from a more primitive period of our history as a science.

To be sure, the weaknesses of an experimental orientation represent only part of the larger conceptual problem of a classical paradigm that was inspired by a mechanistic world view.

Inherent in any consideration of a reshaping of social inquiry should, of course, be a delineation of the proper role of a re-structured method of experimentation. It is clear that experi-mentation does have a place in any new comprehensive scheme; indeed the thrust of the artifact assault was based on the results of experimental investigations. But it is even more important to consider where we are as a field and where we might go. In one of C. P. Snow's novels, a character muses: "what a wonderful invention a map is. Geography would be incomprehensible without maps. They've reduced a tremen-dous muddle of facts into something you can read at a glance."[1] The map for this chapter is Werner Heisenberg's semantic distinction of a closed theory in science, which de-lineates the boundaries of the experimental method and of our naturalistic paradigm and in so doing reveals the larger con-ceptual problem of which the siege on experimentalism is but a part.

The Closed Theory

Isaac Newton developed mathematical laws of mechanics in the seventeenth century which, because of their elegance and precision, became the accepted standards of exact science. In the twentieth century, theoretical advances by Einstein, Hei-senberg, and others exposed the limits of this great compre-hensive formulation of natural laws that had made use of such primary concepts as position, time, velocity, mass, and force. In quantum mechanics, for example, it was necessary to as-sume that certain Newtonian principles when applied to physical microsystems were, in truth, impossibilities.[2] These were not, as Heisenberg has stated rather pointedly, simply minor changes or improvements in the Newtonian laws:

> I think Newtonian mechanics cannot be improved in any way, for inasmuch as we can describe a particular phenomenon with the concepts of Newtonian physics—namely, position, velocity, acceleration, mass, force, etc.—Newton's laws hold quite rigorously, and nothing in this will be changed for the next hundred thousand years.[3]

As a consequence of the revolutionary developments in physics, the realm of the Newtonian theory was now divided among an array of theories, Newton's being one of these.[4] So far as mechanical phenomena can be described by his system of definitions and axioms, which establish the fundamental concepts with a high degree of accuracy, Newtonian physics has an absolute validity within its diminished sphere of application. The conceptual system of Newtonian physics thus constitutes a *closed theory*, Heisenberg argued, in the same way that Maxwell's theory and Einstein's special theory of relativity, modern quantum mechanics, and statistical thermodynamics are specifically contained within the realm of experience they describe. He also detailed three properties belonging to a closed theory which reveal what "content of truth" each of these formulations has.[5]

First, the laws of a closed theory in physics are stated unambiguously; the theory must be logically tight and internally free from contradiction. In Newton's theory, the concepts are specified and fixed in their relations by a system of mathematical equations and precise definitions. Second, the closed theory in physics is directly anchored in experiences that set a decisive limit to its field of application. Beyond the boundaries of these experiences, its concepts and axioms are superseded by some other conceptual scheme. Third, the closed theory in physics contains no perfectly certain statement about the experiential world. Its conceptual limits can never be exactly known, since only the discovery of experiences outside of its jurisdiction may reveal its boundaries. Yet in spite of this uncertainty, these concepts remain a part of the language of science to form a constituency of intellectual presuppositions.[6]

In sum, each closed formulation of natural laws existed for Heisenberg as a closed theory that described a wide realm of experiences, but there were other realms of experience and, therefore, other closed-off formulations as well. Further, each of these comprehensive formulations was recognized as an idealization of reality, which restricted or stylized reality by forgoing all those features that could not be captured by the theory.[7] Is it possible that sociopsychological epistemology is similar to a closed theory?—for it has engendered a consistent idealization of reality and the tools to validate this conception, all of which is circumscribed by a restricted or stylized linguistic frame of reference.[8]

The Notion of a Closed Paradigm

The case for sociopsychological epistemology as a "closed paradigm" proceeds from the assumption that the mechanical conception is a valid basis for the comprehension of certain matters that fall within its theoretical confines, or at least that the method of experimentation is valid for some purposes in social psychology, whether or not we concede the individuality of the human organism. In the following chapter I discuss these purposes, but beyond this theoretical confine there is also a wider range of experiences where other paradigmatic conceptions are required in order to deal with the sweep and purposive character of life. These experiences that cannot be easily integrated into a simple mechanistic framework require a framework of understanding based instead on a psychogenetic or organic or wholistic outlook on social reality. A significant example at this writing has to do with the inability of the mechanistic model to deal with certain conceptual conditions and longitudinal processes for attribution theory within the framework of an experimental orientation.[9] The reason why the method of experimentation is unable to deal with these conditions and processes is that space and time in and of themselves impose limits on the experimental study of life and of social reality.

In spite of this obvious limitation, experimentalism was treated for decades as if its sphere of application was virtually unlimited. For purposes now, and in the following chapter, of delimiting the spatiotemporal boundaries of a naturalistic paradigm, let me begin by distinguishing between two factors that are usually beyond the reach of the method of experimentation, or for that matter of any method that approaches behavior as if it were a constant entity that can be specifically pulled apart and each part then studied in isolation.

There are, first of all, "biocultural influences" at the inter-
face of the subject areas of sociobiology and biosociology. Bio-
culture refers to the biological substratum of social behavior,
although this term can be differentiated from the particular
subject areas of sociobiology and biosociology.[10] Sociobi-
ologists identify two levels of cause: proximate causation, re-
ferring to the internal physiological responses to external
stimuli, and ultimate or distal causation, the way in which
these adaptive proximate mechanisms initially occurred. Of
primary interest to them, however, is the "ultimate cause of
behavior," which, they argue, operates by a species-survival
mechanism—an individual of any species will behave to max-
imize his or her genetic representation in succeeding generations. On the basis of this neo-Darwinian principle, which was
recently made prominent by the theoretical work of Edward
O. Wilson,[11] David P. Barash,[12] and many others, sociobi-
ologists attempt to explain a wide range of behavior, including altruism, incest, jealousy, and so on for all species.[13]
Biosociology refers merely to a subspeciality or a topical area
of sociology, proceeding on the assumption that biology in-
teracts with the social environment to produce patterned social behavior. In contrast, biosociology does not refer to a particular theoretical orthodoxy nor does it place as much emphasis on genetic determinants of behavior. In using the term
biocultural influence, I shall mean the interplay between biology and the sum total of habits of living, learning, performing,
etc. built up by a group within a particular time frame. I in-
tend my use of this term to be sufficiently broad so as to
include genetic influences (the province of sociobiology) as
well as nongenetic biological factors such as gender and racial
effects that are biologically circumscribed but also involve
cultural adaptation (from the realm of biosociology).

Second, there are "sociocultural influences," having to do
with historical changes in symbolic systems. By *socioculture* I
mean the sociotropic nature of historical change, particularly
its influence on language, customs, communication, and dispositions. The most familiar term for this sociocultural influence is *zeitgeist*, meaning "spirit of the age,"[14] a concept that
was seized on by historians and political theorists to argue

that attitudes and behaviors were patterned by the habits of thought that pertain to the culture of a region and period.[15] More recently, a substitute term has been introduced by sociologists and sociodevelopmental psychologists, which is the concept of the *cohort* as a temporal unit in the study of social change; they use it to denote a generation, but in a macroanalytic as opposed to a statistical or demographic sense of a "generation of 20 or 30 years."[16] Thus, we speak of the "postwar generation" or the "lost generation" or the "generation of egocentric anarchy of the 1970s," and know that these terms are each associated with social changes that partly define a period of history and also the beliefs and psychological habits of those born in the same time interval and aging together (hence, cohorts).

Confounding of Intrapersonal Processes

Because the method of experimentation proceeds in terms of relatively immediate or instantaneous states, without regard for the secular or developmental history of individuals, there is a void of understanding with regard to most biocultural and sociocultural influences even at the most fundamental level of human activity, that which is within the individual (including cognitive, perceptual, intellectual, and emotional processes). Suppose that we did an experiment to study some individual capability that was moderated by the impact of historical changes on cohorts (for example the impact of a war or of a new technological achievement). Insofar as these improbable events, which were associated with sociopsychological changes in populations, cannot be experimentally repeated at will (except possibly as analogues), the experimental method in social psychology may be of limited value, and any subsequent empirical generalization about biocultural regularities would be "closed off" by historical circumstances.

There is a well-known nonexperimental example of this confounding of intrapersonal processes and secular time, which served to show how a famous psychological generalization was circumscribed by historical limitations of the original data. For many years it was taught that human intelligence, beginning in early adulthood, declined with age.[17] Evidence for this generalization was based on the results of I.Q. tests which were given at the same time to younger and older persons whose intelligence scores were then correlated with their calendar ages. However, in an analysis of the extensive testing records of military draftees during the First and Second World Wars, it was noted that the mean intelligence of the World War II recruits coincided with the 82nd percentile of the World War I recruits.[18] In other words, if in 1941 both samples had been tested simultaneously, it would have *looked as if* the older sample had lost some intelligence points over the intervening period of 24 years. Although it would have appeared that intelligence, beginning in early adulthood, declined with age, the supposed deficiencies (in retest performance) might just as well be attributed to sociocultural differences in education, child rearing, technological developments in society, etc., between cohorts.[19] Because of these sociocultural differences, the older and younger samples were significantly different initially. But the research design, because it focused on instantaneous states, was insufficient for sorting out the interaction of individual and sociocultural changes.[20]

In this case the original theoretical generalization was proven incorrect. But it is also possible to point to examples in which the validity of the original generalization was unchallenged but its area of application is now redivided among an array of theories. To illustrate: the conception of human cognition that has most recently served as a prototype of cognitive functioning is Leon Festinger's cognitive dissonance theory.[21] The line from a mechanical conception to dissonance theory first twists around W. B. Cannon's classic notions of homeostasis and energy mobilization,[22] Wolfgang Köhler's analysis of the "fittingness of organic change,"[23] and then around various consistency or equilibrium theories of Fritz Heider and others which were liberally derived from the biological-mechanism analogy. The specific notion of Festinger's theory is that there is "a drive toward consonance among cognitions"—that man tries to establish "internal harmony, consistency, or congruity among his opinions, atti-

tudes, knowledge, and values." Such a mechanism is set into
motion, Festinger argues, whenever dissonance exists between two cognitions, when the opposite of one follows from
the other. The dissonance produced by discrepant cognitions
will then function as would any biological drive—if we are
hungry, we do something to reduce our discomfort from it; if
we experience cognitive dissonance, we do something to reduce our discomfort from it. There have, in fact, been
hundreds of experiments to delineate the cognitive domain of
dissonance theory, resulting in a series of revisions theoretically delimiting its immediate realm of application.[24] But be-
sides being restricted to its own specialized domain in the
here and now (aspects of which are amenable to experimental
verification)[25] the theory of cognitive dissonance may be
"closed off" by historical circumstances of acquired personal
responsibility and the emergence of a justificatory or rational-
izing mentality in individuals (sociocultural conditions that
are not susceptible to experimental manipulation). A similar
argument would apply in the case of any cognitive activity
that was only studied in terms of instantaneous states,
whether experimentally or nonexperimentally.[26]

Confounding of Interpersonal Processes

To be sure, there is also a void of understanding with regard
to biocultural and sociocultural influences at higher levels of
human activity, those operating in the interpersonal sphere
(including persuasion and social influence, group dynamics,
manifestations of intergroup prejudices, and various other interpersonal processes). The slice of time may in this case be
more substantial, but in the wider framework of either an historic or teleologic outlook it is still quite narrow.

For example, Gordon W. Allport hypothesized that equal
status interactions between majority and minority groups in
the pursuit of common goals will moderate intergroup prejudices.[27] Allport reasoned that contact, by correcting false perceptions that were formerly the basis of prejudiced attitudes,
would foster more positive attitudes. Some of the more nota-
ble expository research on Allport's principle was done by

Stuart Cook and his associates.[28] In a ten-year research project, they manipulated a number of situational characteristics that they hypothesized could mediate the reduction of intergroup prejudices. For instance, they experimented with encouraging cooperative relationships and with establishing equivalent status settings for an interaction between blacks and whites. In general, these research findings disclosed that a high degree of participation in some joint decision-making effort produced a high level of mutual satisfaction and liking of one another, especially if the joint effort was successful. Other studies of integrated housing during this period also revealed that there was a tendency to change social attitudes toward the norms of the living area, and that cooperative residential contact between blacks and whites served to decrease conflict and prejudice.[29] In a more recent study, interracial attitudes and behavior were observed during a series of week-long sessions at a summer camp for boys and girls 8 to 12 years old. The camp was situated in such a way that each bunk had a black counselor and a white counselor along with equal members of black campers and white campers. The results of these observations were also consistent with Allport's hypothesis, in that there were measurable positive changes on a variety of criteria that reflected the children's improved interracial attitudes and behavior toward one another.[30]

Insofar as McGuire's dictum of the yin and yang of social psychology is plausible ("the opposite of a great truth is also true"),[31] it is possible that the opposite of the equal status interaction hypothesis is also true. But this may not be easily adduced experimentally, since Allport's extrapolation could depend on the temper of the times or the sociocultural context of behavior, which is a given that is not readily accessible to experimental manipulation. Indeed, there have been countless instances throughout history of social contact *and* conflict, in which intergroup attitudes became further polarized within, if not because of, an atmosphere of zealous and belligerent chauvinism. Dalmas A. Taylor has recently developed this theoretical idea in some detail, particularly with respect to majority and minority group contacts in American society.[32] The failure of social scientists to realize the possible contraindicating limitations of excessive devotion to a cause, whether by the majority or the minority group, Taylor argues, has blinded most of us so that we do not see that the positive effects of equal status contact are circumscribed by a changeable cultural and political ecology.

In this one respect, at least, the metatheoretical domain of social inquiry is perhaps no different from other nomothetic sciences that study changeable events. Epidemiologists have come to realize that powerful drugs to combat virulent diseases can sometimes lead to hardier strains of the diseases, which through spontaneous mutations then become immune to the drugs.[33] Is it possible that the diseases of racism and prejudice also require a scientific and theoretical outlook that recognizes that human events are in perpetual flux? By routinely ignoring the temporal and spatial dimensions of human events, we may unwittingly exacerbate reactive events by the very methods devised to treat them.

There are other plausible examples to illustrate how a particular theoretical generalization is enclosed within a biocultural or sociocultural framework in the interpersonal sphere.[34] Edward E. Sampson has speculated on how principles of equity and reciprocity may also be applicable only within a cultural and political frame of reference.[35] Equity, he argues, is specifically congruent with a capitalistic economic system, as exemplified by the American ideal of self-contained individualism. Were our values different, perhaps another kind of motivational norm would have emerged as a cultural ideal. But instead, our contemporary views of mental health also emphasize this self-contained, individualistic ideal. Reciprocity can also be viewed as a specific cultural norm, where the idea of a relationship is explicitly tit-for-tat.[36]

This possible confounding of intra- and interpersonal processes as a consequence of biocultural and sociocultural factors argues to the point that sociopsychological facts may be limited and unrepeatable just to the extent that they are circumscribed by events and secular changes that are beyond the easy reach of methods that foreclose on the dimensions of time and space. I have briefly mentioned in a previous chapter how in nineteenth-century physics there were attempts to construct unitary models of both electricity and ether, but the failure of numerous experiments to detect the motion of the earth relative to the ether eventually led to the conclusion that no mechanical experiment on a physical system could ever reveal whether it was at rest or moving uniformly in a straight line.[37] It also seems true that no experiment on a sociopsychological system can unconfound the interaction of sociocultural and biocultural changes, which instead require a different outlook on social reality. It remains for us now to delineate whatever proper role the experimental method (and similar methods) may have in social inquiry, but at the same time to think of alternatives to the closed-off area of application of a classical mechanistic orientation.

7 Reconstruction of Social Psychology

The fact that social material is less repeatable than that of natural
science, creates greater difficulty in verifying social laws but it
does not abrogate the common ideal of all science. . . . It leaves
us with the conviction that in view of the historical character of
social facts we ought to be especially on guard not to accept as
law that which merely seems to hold true of present or past
social phenomena. The process of distilling the essential law
from social phenomena must be surrounded with many more
cautions than the similar process applied to physical events.

Morris R. Cohen
Reason and Nature

Earlier I discussed how the Enlightenment, and then positivism, produced a vision of science as the court of reason
before which superstition and dogma were conquered by the
gathering of objective, value-free knowledge that purified the
facts and eliminated the human error. Although several centuries separate us from the origin of this idealization of the
scientific method, the social psychology of today is still more
the domain of that antiquated ideal than of conceptions of
modern science. In this chapter I explore some preliminary
steps for the reshaping of social inquiry as a pluralistic
science. To experiment also means *to test* or *to try*, and it is
time that we tested and tried alternative methods with the
same vigor invested in the synchronic methods, particularly
the method of experimentation, that have served psychology
for over a hundred years.

We are beginning to understand very well what these old

methods cannot do, but there is no general consensus among researchers about what they can do. Speaking of the method of experimentation, J. S. Mill in his *Logic* raised the interesting question as to why it is that in some fields one experiment may be decisive while in other fields large numbers of experiments bring no certain results. Morris R. Cohen answered Mill this way:

> In any fairly uniform realm like that of physics, where we can vary one factor at a time, it is possible to have a crucial experiment, that is, it is possible to reduce an issue to a question of yes or no, so that the result refutes and eliminates one hypothesis and leaves the other in possession of the field. But where the number of possible causes is indefinitely large, and where we cannot always isolate a given factor, it is obviously difficult to eliminate an hypothesis; and the elimination of one hypothesis from a very large number does not produce the impression of progress in the establishment of a definite cause.[1]

Whether the "one factor at a time" objection is really relevant to "social" psychology is a debatable point. One can use analysis of variance designs which orthogonally vary three or four independent variables, or one can use multiple regression analysis, multivariate analysis, or structural equation models to deal with many covarying factors all at once. There are also logical as well as methodological justifications for the experiment, and in this chapter I begin by discussing the logical reasons for approaching some problems by the use of experimental methods in social psychology. While we are enroute to a pluralistic science with room for both synchronic and diachronic methods of investigation, it is also imperative to delineate the areas of application of each of these. I then discuss what gaps in theory and method need to be filled if we are ever to achieve this ambitious undertaking.

Domain of Experimentalism

There are several important tasks for which the method of experimentation (carefully reshaped to control for artifacts) seems to be well suited in social psychology. First, it can be used to nullify theoretical generalizations in the form of unqualified negative assertions, by showing instances in which the null hypothesis is specifically refuted. Second, it can provide a pointer reading [2] (an empirical reference point) to support (though not to confirm definitively) a postulated dynamic relationship. Third, it can be used in conjunction with other methods and theory to delimit the subcultural domain of relationships in the here and now.

The first use, that of showing specific instances in which the null hypothesis is false, may be illustrated in very general terms by the experiments that comprised the artifact assault. The negative assertion that had to bear the brunt of this assault was the notion that experimental data were *not* affected by the extraneous influences of the experimenter in any systematic ways. In the classical design, all the variables on the stimulus side are held constant except for the independent variable, x, and effects are then observed on the subject side on the dependent variable, y. However, the artifact assault advanced on the counterassumption that the independent variable in the statement $y = f(x)$ may be contaminated by unspecified determinants that affect the dependent variable systematically. [3] In focusing attentions on the indeterminacy of the specification of what actually constitutes x and *not-x*, the assault also made social psychologists realize that the experiment is more human and subjective than had been originally envisioned.

A specific example to illustrate this point concerned the use of pretests to determine the state of behavior before an experimental manipulation is operational. [4] In testing whether a given manipulation succeeds or not in altering some existing state, it is customary to measure that state before and after the experimental manipulation is tried. However, if the pretest sensitized the respondent to the manipulation, it might, through a focusing of attention, increase or decrease the effect of x on y. Such a possibility was discussed by Donald T. Campbell and Julian C. Stanley, who theorized that, especially in attitude-change studies, where the attitude questionnaire introduces considerable amounts of unusual content, it is plausible that the person's attitudes and susceptibility to persuasion may be influenced to some degree by the prequestionnaire.[5] But because the few published studies on this problem reported no such sensitizing effect, most social psychologists had proceeded on the negative assumption that the act of measuring a person's behavior before manipulating it did not affect the postexperimental state of behavior in any systematic way.[6] This null hypothesis was empirically refuted when it was experimentally shown by Jerry M. Suls and myself how the earlier failure to demonstrate a pretest-by-treatment sensitizing effect was probably due to the fact that motivational differences had been ignored. Once the subjects' volunteer status was taken into account, it could be experimentally demonstrated that there were specific instances in which type I and II errors resulted.[7]

A second use of the method of experimentation in social psychology is to provide empirical reference points that can increase the theoretical impact of a postulated dynamic relationship.[8] The limitation and utility of this application may be illustrated by an analogy from astrophysics.[9] Imagine that we have a mechanical system in space that contains a number of bodies moving with respect to each other, each body exerting a gravitational influence on the others. No dynamic property of this system can be easily determined at any given moment even if we neglect the rest of the universe, because the entire system is in flux. However, it may be possible to develop a set of experiments that generate reference points to show the state of the system at several moments. Social experimentation, in which interventions or reforms are treated as natural experiments, and social indicators are used as pointer readings to document the quality of life, illustrate how in psychology it is also possible to generate pointer readings to show the state of a system at several moments.[10] But these experiments can only provide empirical reference points—they do not have the capacity to forecast changes in the quality of life in trends and tendencies.[11]

A third use of properly controlled experiments would be to mark certain subcultural limits of empirical generalizations in the here and now. To illustrate: during the 1940s a protracted dispute prevailed between Clark L. Hull and Edward C. Tolman over the nature of learning.[12] Hull, inspired by Pavlov's research on conditioned reflexes, had developed a systematic behavior theory which asserted that the stimulus (S) affects the organism (O) but that the resulting response (R) depends upon O as well as upon S. According to this S-O-R model, learning is a mechanistic process, in which S-R connections get automatically strengthened only because they occur in association with reinforcement. Tolman's S-S model (called purposive behaviorism, sign-gestalt theory, or expectancy theory) emphasized the cognitive nature of learning. Behavior is goal-directed and makes use of environmental supports as means-objects toward the goal, but this process is a discontinuous one that depends on exploratory behaviors in which the animal learns what leads to what. Docility, Tolman argued, is thus a mark of purpose, because the animal is learning by acquiring expectations and forming "cognitive maps."

Not only were there distinct theoretical and methodological differences between these two camps, but their results may have been confounded by their use of different "subcultures" of animals having different capabilities or dispositions. The Tolmanians, centered at the University of California, used a strain of rats that had been selectively bred by others from matings of wild males and laboratory albino females. The Hullians, at Yale under Hull's direction and a second camp at Iowa University under Kenneth W. Spence, used another strain of rats that originally had been bred for nonemotionality. The fact that these two "subcultures" of rats had been separated for over thirty years, during which time they had been differently and selectively bred, called into question whether genetic differences could not have played a role in the debate between the Hullians and Tolmanians. An experiment by Marshall B. Jones and Robert S. Fennell, III, was addressed expressly to this question.[13] Jones and Fennell showed empirically that both S-O-R and S-S were theories "closed off" along the biocultural dimension, that the "great debate" over the nature of learning was, in some part, due to genetic differences between the two strains of rats studied by the two camps. To make this point, a sample of rats was obtained from each strain, placed on a 23-hour food or water deprivation schedule, and beginning on the fourth day were given three learning trials daily in a U-maze for ten consecutive days. Specific differences were observed in the performance of the two strains, consistent with the nature of the theoretical differences that separated the two schools of learning. The Hullian rats, in the words of Jones and Fennell, "popped out of the start box, ambled down the runway, around the turn, and into the goal box," while the Tolman rats "seemed almost oblivious to their environment." There were also differences in reported latencies, in that the Tolman rats were recorded as much slower to emerge from the start box and took much more time in the runway proper than did the Hullian rats.

Findings such as these would not necessarily lead us to question the logic or internal consistency of either Hull's or Tolman's theory of learning. But they do raise questions as to the subcultural area of application of Hullian and Tolmanian laws of learning. Learning theorists had experimented in the 1940s as if an empirical resolution of the argument between Hull and Tolman would produce a world formula to establish the basic framework for all learning processes. In actuality, both theories were specifically circumscribed by "subcultural" variables that defined the populations studied. The rationale of doing cross-cultural or cross-national experimental replications in social psychology would proceed along similar theoretical lines in order to mark the cultural limits of empirical generalizations in the here and now.

Theories of Change

Empirical replications done across time, space, and stimulus are science's traditional system of checks and balances to expose or reduce the limits of empirical generalizations. However, replications of sociopsychological experiments across time or subculture would be like a shot in the dark if there were no theoretical grasp of the idea of social change, in part as a consequence of human volition but also as a result of nonvolitional biocultural antecedents.[14] Jones and Fennell's experiment hit the mark because they correctly theorized that Hull's and Tolman's formulations were dependent on the exigencies of variable elements. The task of social psychology is to find theoretical approaches and a range of methods that are sensitive to the exigencies of social change.

There seem to be two possible approaches to this subject, and each has its own group of advocates and dissenters. One possibility is to proceed on the teleological premise of social development, beginning with some pattern of social change to serve as a representational schema. The argument against this approach asserts that the enterprise of rank ordering societies, which is implicit in most theories of social evolution, modernization, or development, is empirically meaningless in our present or foreseeable state of knowledge. The second possibility is to study the dynamics of social change without the baggage of "advancement" as a linguistic and substantive model, as is the case in evolutionary biology which does not attempt to predict the future success of a current adaptation of some species to environment.[15]

If we pursue the first or second alternative, there are at least three further possibilities to consider; that is, three heuristic frameworks within which to search for a degree of theoretical synthesis at an intra- or an interpersonal level of human activity. One plausible pattern that has been discussed recently in sociology is that of a unilinear progression, based on an idealization of the evolutionary tree of life. Another possibility is that of a recursive progression in which social change is characterized by recurrence in cycles. The third possibility, usually called "dialectical," which has also begun to attract some attention in developmental and social psychology, envisions social change as the progressive balancing of opposing forces.[16] Each of these patterns has a long history, and let it suffice here that we consider only their broad outlines. (Beyond these three patterns, there is also the possibility of multilinear progression, in which certain current forms are superior to earlier ones and there are numerous lines of progression so that each current form is relatively optimal for a particular situation.)

The first pattern roughly corresponds to the idea of unilinear advancement in the biological theory of evolution and development. Darwinism argues that there is a constant struggle for species survival in which the most successful evolutionary modifications are those that survive. In a similar vein, the evolutionary model of social change argues that there is a continuous developmental adaptation to the environment by individuals and human societies by means of certain integrating agencies of selection and cultural mutation. This pattern of emergent evolutionism, visualized as a unilinear progression, is seen as orderly and gradual rather than explosive and chaotic. That societies move inexorably through a fixed series of stages, perhaps in the same way that organisms advance up the evolutionary ladder, is a recurrent theme in the writings of August Comte, Herbert Spencer, Wilhelm Wundt, V. Gordon Childe, C. Lloyd Morgan, Emile Durkheim, and many modern theorists in social archeology and cultural anthropology, who have envisioned patterns of social change in which primitive cultures of great simplicity evolved into cultures of ever-increasing societal complexity and interrelatedness.

For example, Comte felt that the progress of civilization resulted "from the instinctive tendency of the human race to perfect itself,"[17] but he also thought that the prevailing order was the proper ideal of human society. For Comte, civilization as a whole, as well as the various components of knowledge and belief that are the cornerstones of society, progress according to a "law of three stages"—which Sorokin later renamed the ideational, the idealistic, and the sensate. Wundt, on the other hand, proposed that there were four stages or periods in the development of civilization. The first stage, that of primitive man, was defined as the lowest grade of culture, including mental culture, although there was no specific ethnological characteristic that distinguished this stage from those that were more advanced. The second stage, the totemic age, was characterized by a reversal in the relations of dominance between humans and animals, in which the animal had dominion over the human being. The third stage was called the age of heroes and gods, which was a higher level of development beginning with a rulership of individuals within the tribal organization and ultimately progressing into the State.

The fourth stage was that of a national State and a national religion, which would then broaden into humanistic associations. These kinds of broad demarcations may be too nebulous to be of much use to most social psychologists. However, the underlying theme of social evolution as a unitary progression has been found useful by some modern researchers.

One recent variation on this essentially teleologic theme is the sociobiological thesis which argues that aspects of social behavior are biologically determined—for example, altruistic behavior that is self-destructive while benefiting another. The explanation for how altruism could possibly have evolved by natural selection was first conceived by W. D. Hamilton, who named it kinship theory.[18] Imagine that two animals have mated and reproduced and that their offspring, being at first helpless to protect themselves, will have to depend on the benevolence of their parents for protection. Babies that will have the greatest chance of surviving the perils of infancy would be those whose parents were altruistic, who will be willing to sacrifice themselves for the benefit of their kin. Thus, the biological influence of kinship (the possession of a common ancestor in the not too distant past) would affect social behavior, even though the altruist makes less of a solitary contribution to the gene pool as the price of his or her self-sacrificial act.

There is, to be sure, an obvious danger if one treats the idea of social evolution as an ontological rather than as a representational process. The difficulty with this position is that it introduces a certain biological inflexibility, dominated once again by mechanistic ideas, unless one allows for a decisive influence of environmental factors in determining growth. The secular, conservative philosophy embraced by earlier social Darwinists, such as Spencer, W. G. Sumner, and others in the late nineteenth and earlier twentieth centuries, required a rigid adherence to the physicalistic notion which attributed social change to everything except human control, as if social determinism were an ontological argument.[19] Some modern structuralists outside of the sociobiological camp also appear to proceed on the assumption that there is an unvarying unilinear succession of universal stages in the advancement of social behavior.[20] Jean Piaget, the eminent developmentalist, may be counted among these theorists, inasmuch as he has contended that intellectual development advances by a universal and invariable sequence of mental stages.[21] Others, however, take unilinear progression merely as a representational theme, to argue for an evolutionary pattern of gradual and orderly progression. For example, Colin Martindale has developed (and empirically explored) an "evolutionary theory" of artistic and literary change. He argues that the constant pressure for change in the art world and the countervailing pressures against it lead to monotonically increasing changes in the arts.[22] This notion that art progresses is, of course, different from the classic idea that the arts and sciences differ in that the arts are noncumulative (that is, Hellenic or Renaissance art might be equally great on aesthetic grounds, only stylistically different) while science cumulates (so that Einstein's science is not only different from Newton's but superior to it).

In contrast to the principle of unilinear growth and adaptation,[23] there is an alternative metaphor or a second pattern that envisions social change as a cyclic (yet developmental) process of genesis and decay. This conception found its most systematic theoretical expression during the eighteenth century in the work of the Italian historian and philosopher Giambattista Vico. His early philosophical leanings were in the rationalistic tradition of Descartes, but Vico's own strongly humanistic attitude soon led him away from the Cartesian viewpoint (the evidential focus of which he considered too narrow) and, in 1725, Vico published his cyclical conception of human nature and human society in his magnum opus, *Scienza nuova*.[24] In this remarkable book he treated culture as an adaptive mechanism to show the complex evolution and devolution of societies conditioned by the structure of the collective mind. A new science was needed, he argued, one that would be sensitive to how qualities of human nature, including language, social customs, civil law, and political institutions were dependent on the "course and recourse" of certain identifiable circumstances. In a similar vein, more recent sociological theories articulated by Oswald Spengler, Pitirim Sorokin, F. Stuart Chapin, and Max Weber also have envisioned an oscillation of social changes as a consequence of historical periods of growth and decline.[25]

How could cyclic change be a progressive process? Think of the ways in which a deciduous tree undergoes systematic changes over its lifetime, progressing from a seedling to a sapling to a mature tree, while at the same time experiencing seasonal changes in which the leaves grow and then die. This recursive evolution, however, is conceived as a representational theme, recognizing that social events may wax and wane because of conflicts and crises that are exacerbated or ameliorated by human endeavors. The cycle synchronies may be inevitable in some respects, but it is nevertheless possible to exert some human influence on social processes that are responsive to historical periodicities, just as it is possible by human means to influence the dynamic properties of the recurrent growth patterns of a tree.[26]

Illustrative of recent empirical reports of cycles or social periodicities is William McGuire's finding that fame in different broad fields of endeavor (government, religion, arts, and literature) has alternately waxed and waned in each century of the past 2,500 years as a function of historical events.[27] The cyclical reappearance of some rumors is also consistent with this second pattern of social change. For example, from the twelfth to the twentieth centuries, there were many instances in which a ritual-murder rumor was laid against the Jews near the time of Passover. The ritual-murder charge was first directed against the Jews some centuries before Christ, when it was rumored that it was customary for Jews to kidnap Greeks, fatten them up, and then offer them in a ritual sacrifice and eat their flesh. Cyclic rumors of sacramental baby-killing and baby-eating were also made against the early Christians. These insidious tales seem to feed on perpetual fears, prejudices, hatreds, and misunderstandings that combine with contemporary stresses that may appear in cycles.[28] Carl G. Jung also noted the cyclical reappearance of certain "visionary rumors," such as stories of flying saucers or unknown aerial objects, as if in response to the *zeitgeist*.[29] By far the most extensive evidence of cyclical trends was that gathered by Edward R. Dewey, founder of the *Journal of Cycle*

Research, who reported cycle synchronies for a wide range of biological and sociological events.[30]

A third possible pattern of social change is based on the principle of polarity, going all the way back to Aristotle's golden mean. What separates this notion from the equilibrium model is the further assumption of dialectical conflict and resolution. The most prominent example of this theoretical perspective in modern philosophy is the dialectical concept of G.W.F. Hegel, Karl Marx, and more recently the Frankfurt School.[31] Hegel's dialectical method of understanding proceeded on the idea that there is a continuous process of canceling out or annulling opposing forces in a higher synthesis that is a blend of the old and the new. Both Hegel and Marx ascribed this dialectical process to history in a utopian manner, arguing that there is a progressive surpassing of ideational clashes inherent in any level of social achievement toward a less alienated and less irrational emergent level. Certain theoretical conceptualizations of the self or ego, especially aspects of Freudian theory, also emphasize this dialectical interdependence of oppositional forces in the developmental process (eros and thanatos, or the id, ego, and superego). Hegel also recognized very well, as had Vico, the historical and cultural influence on thought:

> But men do not at certain epochs merely philosophize in general, for there is a definite philosophy which arises among a people, and the definite character of the standpoint of thought is the same character which permeates all the other historical sides of the spirit of the people, which is most intimately related to them, and which constitutes their foundation. The particular form of a philosophy is thus contemporaneous with a particular constitution of the people amongst whom it makes its appearance, with their institutions and forms of government, their social morality, their societal life and the capabilities, customs and enjoyments of the same.[32]

Some contemporary philosophers, such as Jean-Paul Sartre, in his Critique de la raison dialectique, appear to deny the teleological aspect of a utopian dialectic of history, by radically restricting the scope of the Hegelian and Marxist notion.[33] There are also liberal sprinklings of this more constricted thesis in sociology to explain the processes and products of social change. Neil J. Smelser has recently theorized how society can be conceived as a dialectical interdependence of opposites, a complicated network of "continuously generated and regenerated tensions, strains, contradictions, and pressures to change."[34]

Other recent examples in psychology include Heinz Werner's psychogenetic principle of spirality, which was directly derived from Hegel's thesis concerning the survival of lower levels of functioning in the course of development.[35] Klaus F. Riegel introduced the dialectical thesis most forcefully in his essay on the dependencies of growth upon opposed sociocultural contingencies, such as the clash of economic and political ideologies.[36] Robert E. Lana has also drawn on this thesis to argue that a reconciliation of contradictory hypothetical propositions is the idealized model of experimental inquiry in psychology, but the true dialectical method really goes beyond the structure of an experiment to permit naturally occurring ambivalences.[37]

Empirical Methods

Were social psychology's experimental history nearly as long as its philosophical past, then the corpus of experimental findings might permit us to look in retrospect for social changes corresponding to these representational patterns. (We have, of course, no exact analogy in human social psychology to the comparison of species in evolutionary biology, unless one tries to make the misguided case, which I certainly do not, that cross-cultural comparisons of experimental findings might somehow serve this purpose.) It is encouraging to note that there seems to be growing theoretical interest in tailoring statistical methods to fit integrated results of independent replications, in order to identify transhistorical regularities and longitudinal patterns of social change.[38] Even over a short period of several decades, there may be sufficient data to detect primitive changes suggesting the historical frame of a particular empirical generalization.

An excellent example to illustrate this approach is the recent work by Harris M. Cooper applying meta-analysis to the question of whether there are sex differences in degree of conformity.[39] Cooper's discussion of the limitations and the practical advantages of statistical combinations of independent studies also provides a good introduction to this approach presented as an alternative way to review literature in social psychology. Another prominent example has recently come to light as a consequence of a comprehensive literature review done by Alice H. Eagly in the area of sex differences in influenceability.[40] Textbooks in social psychology and attitude had long asserted that women were more easily influenced, therefore more persuasible and conforming, than men. The usual theoretical interpretation was that this sex difference was due to socialization processes that had taught men to be independent thinkers, a cultural value that was seldom suggested as suitable for women. Eagly, however, uncovered a pronounced difference in the distribution of experimental findings when she compared studies published before 1970 with those published during the period of the women's movement in the 1970s. In contrast to the older experiments that showed significantly greater influenceability among females, the newer studies showed few if any significant sexual differences in influenceability. This suggests that the historical period during which an experiment on sex differences in influenceability is conducted is apparently a major determinant of the likelihood of obtaining results demonstrating that women are more influenceable than men. In this case, empirical support is provided for Kenneth Gergen's social-psychology-as-history notion.

However, new methods of investigation are clearly needed in order to make claim to a wider area of theoretical application in social psychology. The following figure, adapted from recent work of Matilda White Riley and Edward E. Nelson, shows the four broad types into which research designs in social psychology may be classified.[41] It also pinpoints the methodological gaps that need to be filled by developing methods to study stability and social change (sections *b*, *c*, and *d*).

SPATIAL CONFIGURATION

	Entity	System
Synchronic	(a) an independent, self-contained sociopsychological entity, with emphasis on the static rather than the dynamic state of the entity.	(b) a sociopsychological system conditioned by biocultural and sociocultural changes, but with emphasis on the static rather than the dynamic state of the system.
Diachronic	(c) an independent, self-contained sociopsychological entity observed from a teleologic or historic outlook	(d) a sociopsychological system that is conceptualized as being conditioned, in part, by biocultural and sociocultural changes

TIME SPAN

The dimension labeled Time Span refers to the period of observation of a phenomenon in the course of individual or historical development. A phenomenon can be observed as it exists at one brief period in time, not using information about the span of individual or historical development (*synchronic*), or it can be observed in such a way as to uncover changes between successive periods of time (*diachronic*). The other dimension, Spatial Configuration, refers to whether a phenomenon is treated as an independent and self-contained *entity* or as a complex, potentially changeable *system*. To the extent that it is possible to compartmentalize research methods and modes of thinking, I would say that the method of experimentation and experimentalism would be relegated to section *a* (like the survey method in sociology). That is because the experiment, as indeed any transverse method, places the empirical emphasis on the relatively immediate or static state of a phenomenon, rather than its dynamic state, and treats the object of study as an isolated entity rather than as a system conditioned by patterns of contextual changes (the basis of artifacts), by biocultural and sociocultural changes, or by improbable events which cannot be studied in laboratories. The optimum method, or combination of methods, would fall in section *d*, which is congruent with a model of social change on both dimensions.[42]

Some promising empirical advances in the diachronic mode

have recently been made, which might be pursued further in a spirit of methodological pluralism in social psychology. For example, the potential for testing sociopsychological hypotheses with cross-era data has been explored by McGuire, who with coworkers has also begun to build an historical data archive.[43] There are, of course, many archival sources and demographic data files in sociology and economics for tracking social changes. Another investigator who has recently done extensive research along this line, using time-series designs to study the unfolding of sociopsychological processes, is Dean Keith Simonton.[44] McGuire points out that the modern derivation of this empirical orientation to historical comparisons has its roots in the work of Sorokin in the 1930s, J. Richardson and Kroeber in the 1940s, and others in more recent decades.[45] Applying cross-lag analysis to tease causality out of relational observations, McGuire and Simonton lead the way in social psychology in showing how it may be possible to test temporal sequences in the appearance of innovations in cultural forms and social organizations.

Simonton, using a transhistorical design that is a variation on the strong-inference method of experimentation, looked at the problem of the causal relation between intellectual and political movements.[46] In this quasi-experiment, he matched David McClelland's well-known hypothesis, which explains the ascent and decline of civilizations in terms of personal needs and values, against Pitirim Sorokin's view that personal beliefs are a response to prevailing political and cultural events. The unit of analysis was a twenty-year time interval or generation. The sample consisted of 122 consecutive generations of European history, from 540 B.C. to A.D. 1900, for which there were observations available on measures of philosophical beliefs and political context. Using the logic of cross-lag analysis, Simonton reasoned that if variation in a political variable always preceded variation in a philosophical variable, then personal beliefs are probably a function of sociocultural context (Sorokin's conclusion). But if variation in a philosophical variable always preceded variation in a political variable, then personal beliefs may possess sociocultural consequences (McClelland's conclusion). Simonton has reported evidence of both causal patterns, depending on the particular circumstances of the variables surveyed, which points to an interaction between individual and society.

In other studies Simonton has again resorted to a diachronic mode of thought to study this causal interaction between individual and society, and to evaluate their respective contributions.[47] For example, he has recently examined the individual and situational factors that affected the final military decision of hundreds of land battles. He has empirically shown that the "great genius theory" (of Thomas Carlyle) as well as the *zeitgeist* notion each contain explanatory value for understanding factors such as casualty rates, tactical victories, and other significant aspects of military successes on the battlefield. Diachronic analyses such as these should sensitize us to the idea that sociopsychological relations circumscribed by temporal variables may be beyond the reach of traditional synchronic methods, which essentially foreclose on the temporal orientation and define phenomena as self-contained entities rather than as part of a larger social configuration. Social psychologists would also stand to benefit by thorough familiarity with recent cohort work in the life-span development area, both on methodological and conceptual grounds.

Even within the synchronic frame of an experimental orientation, however, there are certainly ways of improving the research by solidifying the area of application. These would include using procedures for reducing artifact influences in the laboratory,[48] looking for long-term effects following experimental treatments,[49] using multiple dependent measures,[50] programming the environment over extended time periods,[51] and using methods that can identify diffusion effects and structural reorganizations which may be postulated from diachronic theories.[52,53]

Of greater necessity in social psychology, to be sure, is the urgency to study human activities in social-structural terms that are not dependent only on a synchronic mode of thought, but are also dependent on kinetic or diachronic measurements using time as a parameter. The development of cohort and structural analysis, methods of exploratory data analysis, spectral analytic methods, and quasi-experimental methods, despite their limitations at present, are important steps in the direction of developing alternative methods for the analysis of social change and stability over time.[54] Because of the wide interest among sociologists, quantitative historians, and macro-economists in the study of change and stability, other innovative diachronic methods now being tried in these fields may also be adapted for quantitative use in social psychology.

There is also a growing literature consisting of synchronic qualitative methods for the study of embedded social structures.[55] From simple biographical analysis to a systematic procedure for adducing thematic elements in concepts and methods, there is an expanding body of work in which qualitative research methods have been introduced in social science. An example at this writing is the sociological approach known as ethnomethodology which, in its emphasis on the relationship between contexts and particulars, represents a distinct qualitative advance in the conceptualization of social activities as situated or embedded events rather than as independent entities to be experimentally isolated in the social psychologist's laboratory.[56] By triangulating on the findings of multiple methods, including both quantitative and qualitative methods, we may with an increasing degree of certainty establish the structures of complex social systems that are conditioned by biocultural and sociocultural changes.

However, in spite of our keen interest in using the most rigorous methods to study social phenomena as systems conditioned by complex environmental influences, we must also realize that there are, and perhaps always will be, theoretical endeavors that go beyond the methodology available for their investigation. Contrary to popular empiricism, which speaks as if any respectable theory must be immediately and definitively testable, there must also be room for theories that reach beyond the existing methodology.[57] Diachronic theories seem far more important in the long run than methods, and we must look to such theories to pull innovative methods along with them rather than acquiesce to the confinements imposed by the currently available methodology.

8 Review and Conclusions

> It is often said that behavioral science should stop trying to imitate physics. I believe that this recommendation is a mistake . . . What *is* important, I believe, is that behavioral science should stop trying to imitate only what a particular reconstruction claims physics to be.
>
> Abraham Kaplan
> *The Conduct of Inquiry*

Give a small child a hammer, and the child will find that everything needs pounding. Abraham Kaplan has called this the law of the instrument.[1] It is also a way of looking at a very human trait of individual scientists and characterizes the way in which the method of experimentation took hold in social psychology. The mechanical conception of natural science became an ideal to be imitated in psychological epistemology, and scientific laboratories for the experimental investigation of psychological processes sprung into being in Europe and in the United States a hundred years ago. Applied to social psychology, the tools of experimental psychology seemed to be the perfect implements for the discovery and comprehension of complex social phenomena. Give a discipline in its most formative years a method of experimentation, and the researchers will soon find that everything needs experimenting. By the middle of this century, the experimental method had become the exemplar of scientific methodology in social psychology and a synchronic mode of thought the norm.

Interestingly, even while mechanics was being propounded three centuries ago, some of its assumptions were already being questioned by Leibniz, who envisaged a relativistic cosmology that considered space as merely a congruity of physical objects (as opposed to something with its own independent existence).[2] It is intriguing to contemplate what psychology might have become had an alternative thesis prevailed during this period.[3] The conception of a world in flux is given in *Ecclesiastes*,[4] and there are still embryonic fragments of an organic or wholistic doctrine in several modern theories that stress progressive change as a teleological relationship.[5] The earliest and most systematic development of this diachronic notion in social philosophy was in Vico's profound essay *Scienza nuova*, published in the eighteenth century.

But no matter what might have been, the most influential scientists and philosophers of this period arrived at conceptions drawn from Newtonian mechanics that have haunted us right to the present. Central to eighteenth-century experimentalism was the approach to the experimental method, for it was felt that nature could be understood by imitating it in the laboratory. This idea—later used as a justification for psychological epistemology—was based on the notion of the simplicity of nature, by which was meant that similar effects (whether produced in the laboratory or by nature) had the same causes.[6] Of Vico's call for a New Science and of his theory of cycle synchronies in social evolution, H. P. Adams writes: "It was as if a great ship had been built, capable of navigating all the oceans of the world, and was left moored in the dock of the shipbuilder to be visited occasionally by a few friends of the inventor, and mentioned in their correspondence by one or two superior persons who recognized not so much its value as the cleverness that must have gone to its construction."[7]

Just as the experimental revolution began as an erosion of confidence in the authority of the written word, the modern revolution in social psychology started as an erosion of trust in the authority of experimentalism. The psychic scars left by societal events in the 1960s unleashed a torrent of anxiety about the authority of institutionalized ideals in all fields, and the romanticized vision of scientific objectivity was one such assumption that declined in esteem. Scientists in all fields soon began talking about the critical limits of scientific inquiry, instead of treating science as an endless frontier. It seemed that in every field there was now a crisis of confidence, at the root of which was this erosion of trust in classical postulates. For example, in mathematics it became apparent that the limits of intelligence also imposed barriers even on theoretically decidable questions, and that mathematicians would have to learn to live in a limbo of uncertainty in which formerly invincible methods of proof were now obsolete. In philosophy it became clear that causal relationships need not be law-like, and further that the hypothetico-deductive method, which was based on the syllogism, simply could not be sustained by formal logic if there was allowance made for probabilistic conclusions.[8] Similar crises of confidence seemed to infect all fields, from physics and mathematics to philosophy, biomedicine, and sociology, as scientists began questioning the fundamental verities of modern science.

Social psychology was no exception to this assault on epistemological assumptions, which in the 1960s and 1970s were attacked from all quarters. Not only was the earlier romantic myth and the new realistic view of experimental psychology brought into sharp contrast, but the siege on experimentalism laid waste to the classical thesis that denied there were any important differences in the methods appropriate to studying complex societies and nature. Thus, no longer do we harbor illusions concerning the objectivity of a positivistic orientation, for we know that there are, or can be, biases in the interpretation of data stemming from the ways in which psychologists of different political ideologies or different cultural or biographical backgrounds fulfill their scientific roles. We also know that there are norms and counternorms in all sciences, and that much of what classical philosophy asserted as characteristic of science has been negated by the history of science.[9]

Classical philosophy introduced into epistemology a rigid distinction between the world of appearances and the objective reality underlying these appearances. Truth, it was maintained, consisted of an adequate conception of, or correspondence with, reality. Later, philosophers assumed a more flexible posture in contending that ascriptions of truth, which presupposed the resolution of relevant doubts, always depended on societal norms and expectations. To be relevant for appraising the justifiability of our beliefs, these doubts must be formulable.[10] The advances against experimentalism first put social psychologists in a position to make their doubts formulable as quite particular challenges to the truth of what they formerly believed. The artifact assault taught them that the psychological experiment was more human and subjective than once believed. It also made them think that perhaps indeterminacy attends the study of complex societies and of human nature, just as in modern physics there is a suspicion that matter is ultimately undetermined. The value assault demolished illusions concerning the moral neutrality of experimentalism, and in social psychology it became clear that, like any human endeavor, our scientific enterprise is fed by a wellspring of personal values, prejudices, motives, and goals that, in turn, are infused with illusions and self-delusions. The methods of social psychology, as indeed all human processes, were realized to be interdependent parts of a changeable social system that is influenced by cultural and political values, substantive preconceptions, and professional values and norms.

Although it is true that certain psychological processes or events can be adequately investigated by experimental methods, it is also clear that the classical view of Titchener and others claiming that the method of scientific inquiry must be experimental is an oversimplification based on an exaggerated conception of human character and of the power of this particular method. Social phenomena, unlike mechanical objects, do not remain indifferent to biocultural and sociocultural influences which produce an environment that is in constant flux. William McGuire has observed, "In science as in agriculture, it is well to allow a heavily worked field to lie fallow from time to time while we cultivate other neglected areas."[11] It is indeed time to foster a dialogue of ideas about the domain of experimentalism, to encourage the development of diachronic procedures that go beyond a synchronic area of application, and to cultivate other neglected areas. Various procedures will need to be tried over a long period and the faulty ones eliminated in order to find the best methods to attain the desired results within a specified area. We must not close our minds against other innovative theories and methods that are outside the jurisdiction of a synchronic mode of inquiry, for the disillusionment prevalent in social psychology can be exploited to stimulate the development of an array of admissible paradigms and a constructive reshaping of theoretical interstices.

Isaiah Berlin, in his essay *The Hedgehog and the Fox*, drew on a line among the fragments of the Greek poet Archilochus which says: "The fox knows many things, but the hedgehog knows one big thing." [12] Like Dante, Plato, Hegel, and Nietzsche, there are great thinkers, Berlin argued, whose intellectual and artistic personality belongs to the "hedgehogs"— because they relate everything to a single central vision. Others, including Shakespeare, Aristotle, and Goethe, belong to the "foxes"—because they pursue many ends or visions that are centrifugal rather than centripetal and move on many levels rather than on a single coherent level. For many years, social psychology has also belonged to the hedgehogs, committed to a unitary vision of science with the dogged determination of one who is possessed with a universal organizing principle of all human experience. However, the crisis of experimentalism has created an urgency for social psychology to move on many levels instead of the single paradigmatic level that has been tested and found wanting. The time is ripe to liberate social psychology from the mind-set of an outmoded or exaggerated paradigm and reduce our dependence on the quick-fix of using synchronic methods to try to answer all questions at every level of human activity. Like the hedgehog, social psychology must see the exigencies of social change, which emerges so clearly as a unitary theme. But like the fox, it must begin to pursue a methodological and theoretical pluralism that makes it possible to deal with social change and stability at all levels of human activity.

Notes
and References

1 A Paradigm in Perspective

1. T. S. Kuhn, *The Structure of Scientific Revolutions* (Chicago: University of Chicago Press, 1962). For a discussion of paradigms and psychological epistemology, see also W. Weimer, *Notes on the Methodology of Scientific Research* (Hillside, N.J.: Erlbaum, 1979).
2. See, for example, the following discussions concerning these commonalities shared by psychologists: M. Gergen, "Biographical Indicators of a Paradigmatic Science," Unpublished paper, Temple University Department of Psychology, 1977; N. Levine, "On the Metaphysics of Social Psychology: A Critical View," *Human Relations*, 1976, vol. 29, pp. 385–400; L. Petrinovich, "Probabilistic Functionalism: A Conception of Research Method," *American Psychologist*, 1979, vol. 34, pp. 373–390.
3. For the wider implications of this notion outside of physics, see M. R. Cohen, *Reason and Nature: An Essay on the Meaning of Scientific Method* (New York: Dover, 1978), pp. 247f. (originally published by Harcourt, Brace, 1931).
4. For popular discussion of Kuhn's views on this, see N. Wade, "Thomas S. Kuhn: Revolutionary Theorist of Science," *Science*, 1977, vol. 197, pp. 143–145.
5. By *experimentalism* I mean both the practice of relying on experiments (usually laboratory experimental manipulations) to confirm or refute propositions set forth as an explanation for complex psychological or sociopsychological phenomena as well as a reductionistic, materialistic, linear process doctrine as a conceptual approach.
6. K. Danziger, "The Positivist Repudiation of Wundt," *Journal of the History of the Behavioral Sciences*, 1979, vol. 15, pp. 205–230.

7. E. B. Titchener, *Systematic Psychology: A Prolegomena* (Ithaca, N.Y.: Cornell University Press, 1972), p. 70 (originally published by Macmillan, 1929).
8. See also discussion by Cohen, as cited, pp. 294f.
9. See, for example, discussions of this point by A. O. Lovejoy, *The Great Chain of Being: A Study of the History of an Idea* (Cambridge, Mass.: Harvard University Press, 1936); T. Verhave and W. van Hoorn, "The Temporalization of Ego and Society During the Nineteenth Century: A View From the Top," *Annals New York Academy of Sciences,* 1976, pp. 140–148.
10. A. Einstein and L. Infeld, *The Evolution of Physics: The Growth of Ideas From Early Concepts to Relativity and Quanta* (New York: Simon & Schuster, 1938), pp. 57–58.
11. S. C. Pepper, *World Hypotheses: A Study in Evidence* (Berkeley: University of California Press, 1972). Cohen, as cited. H. W. Reese and W. F. Overton, "Models of Development and Theories of Development," in P. Baltes and L. Goulet, eds., *Life Span Developmental Psychology: Research and Theory* (New York: Academic Press, 1970). W. F. Overton and H. W. Reese, "Models of Development: Methodological Implications," in J. Nesselroad and H. W. Reese, eds., *Life Span Developmental Psychology* (New York: Academic Press, 1973).
12. Einstein and Infeld, as cited, p. 6.
13. A. C. Elms, "The Crisis of Confidence in Social Psychology," *American Psychologist,* 1975, vol. 30, pp. 967–976.
14. See also G. C. Homans, "What Kind of a Myth is the Myth of a Value-Free Science," *Social Science Quarterly,* 1978, vol. 58, pp. 530–541; R. K. Merton, "Science and Democratic Social Structure," in R. K. Merton, ed., *Social Theory and Social Structure* (New York: Free Press, 1968), pp. 604–615.
15. See also discussions by D. Bakan, *On Method: Toward a Reconstruction of Psychological Investigation* (San Francisco: Jossey Bass, 1967); R. Harré and P. F. Secord, *The Explanation of Social Behaviour* (Oxford: Blackwell, 1972).
16. For general discussion of this idea, see R. L. Rosnow, "Experimental Artifact," in *Encyclopedia of Education* (New York: Free Press and Macmillan, 1971), vol. 3, pp. 483–488; R. L. Rosnow, "Social Research: Artifacts," in *International Encyclopedia of Psychiatry, Psychology, Psychoanalysis, and Neurology* (New York: Aesculapius, 1977), vol. 10, pp. 328–331.
17. M. T. Orne, "The Nature of Hypnosis: Artifact and Essence," *Journal of Abnormal and Social Psychology,* 1959, vol. 58, pp.

277–299; M. T. Orne, "On the Social Psychology of the Psychological Experiment: With Particular Reference to Demand Characteristics and Their Implications," *American Psychologist*, 1962, vol. 17, pp. 776–783.

18. R. Rosenthal, "Projection, Excitement, and Unconscious Experimenter Bias," *American Psychologist*, 1958, vol. 13, pp. 345–346; R. Rosenthal, *Experimenter Effects in Behavioral Research* (New York: Appleton-Century-Crofts, 1966); R. Rosenthal and K. L. Fode, "The Problem of Experimenter Outcome-Bias," in D. P. Ray, ed., *Series Research in Social Psychology* (Washington, D. C.: National Institute of Social and Behavioral Science, 1961), Symposia studies series no. 8.

19. R. Rosenthal, "Covert Communication in the Psychological Experiment," *Psychological Bulletin*, 1967, vol. 67, pp. 356–367.

20. I. Silverman, "Crisis in Social Psychology: The Relevance of Relevance," *American Psychologist*, 1971, vol. 26, pp. 583–584.

21. Titchener, as cited, p. 30.

22. See discussion by L. Marx, "Reflections on the Neo-Romantic Critique of Science," in G. Holton and R. S. Morison, eds., *Limits of Scientific Inquiry* (New York: Norton, 1978), pp. 61–74.

23. See, for example, discussion by H. C. Kelman, *A Time to Speak* (San Francisco: Jossey Bass, 1968).

24. For presentation of the complete program of research, see S. Milgram, *Obedience to Authority: An Experimental View* (New York: Harper & Row, 1974).

25. G. Holton, "From the Endless Frontier to the Ideology of Limits," in G. Holton and R. S. Morison, eds., *Limits of Scientific Inquiry* (New York: Norton, 1978), pp. 227–241.

26. K. J. Gergen, "Social Psychology as History," *Journal of Personality and Social Psychology*, 1973, vol. 26, pp. 309–320; K. J. Gergen, "Social Psychology, Science, and History," *Personality and Social Psychology Bulletin*, 1976, vol. 2, pp. 373–383. See earlier discussion by Cohen, as cited, pp. 351f.

27. W. J. McGuire, "The Yin and Yang of Progress in Social Psychology: Seven Koan," *Journal of Personality and Social Psychology*, 1973, vol. 26, pp. 446–456, quoted from p. 448.

28. I am aware that some have argued that the extent of our prescientific knowledge of human behavior essentially precludes even the possibility that the kind of paradigm shift that occurred in physics can ever occur in psychology. Scriven argues that we begin with too much knowledge about human behavior for our concepts of human nature to be radically altered. See M. Scriven,

"Views of Human Nature," in T. Wann, ed., *Behaviorism and Phenomenology* (Chicago: University of Chicago Press, 1964). But there are, of course, concepts of human nature that *have* shifted; see discussion by I. Berlin, *Vico and Herder: Two Studies in the History of Ideas* (New York: Vintage Books, 1976).

29. Kuhn, as cited. Wade, as cited.
30. Verhave and van Hoorn, as cited.
31. Einstein and Infeld, as cited, p. 311.
32. For popular discussion on this point, see A. Einstein, "On the Generalized Theory," *Scientific American*, 1950, vol. 209, pp. 3–7.
33. W. Heisenberg, *Across the Frontiers* (New York: Harper & Row, 1974). W. Heisenberg, *Physics and Beyond: Encounters and Conversations* (New York: Harper & Row, 1971).
34. F. J. Dyson, "Mathematics in the Physical Sciences," *Scientific American*, 1964, vol. 211, pp. 129–146.
35. There is some controversy over whether Einstein really adhered to the tenets of positivism or not, and whether he *operationally defined* coordinate time. See discussion by E. Zahar, who argues that had Einstein adhered to Mach's philosophy of science, then special relativity would never have been formulated. Article by Zahar is "Mach, Einstein, and the Rise of Modern Science," *British Journal of the Philosophy of Science*, 1977, vol. 28, pp. 195–213.
36. Heisenberg, *Across the Frontiers*, as cited.

2   The Rise of Experimentalism

1. For discussion, see, for example, W. A. Wallace, *Causality and Scientific Explanation: Medieval and Early Classical Science* (Ann Arbor: University of Michigan Press, 1972).
2. For longer excerpt from *Opus maius*, see anthology edited by S. Sambursky, *Physical Thought: From the Presocratics to the Quantum Physicists: An Anthology* (New York: Pica Press, 1975), p. 155.
3. Wallace, as cited, pp. 49–50. W. S. Fowler, *The Development of Scientific Method* (Oxford: Pergamon, 1962), p. 36.
4. Quoted from C.E.K. Mees, "Scientific Thought and Social Reconstruction," *Electrical Engineering*, 1934, vol. 53, pp. 383f.
5. Implications for psychological epistemology are discussed by R. Lowry, "Galilean and Newtonian Influences on Psychological Thought," *American Journal of Psychology*, 1969, vol. 82, pp. 391–400.

6. Wallace, as cited.
7. Sambursky, as cited, p. 174.
8. That the objects were dropped from the Leaning Tower of Pisa is apocryphal.
9. This theorem stated: "If the object on which we stand is moved all our movements and those of things movable by us happen and appear just as though it were stationary." Quoted from Sambursky, as cited, p. 255.
10. Among other Galilean influences on psychological thought was his reflexive cosmology of matter-in-motion, which was later seized on by Hobbes as the basis for a biological analogy: "What is the heart, but a spring; and the nerves, but so many strings; and the joints so many wheels, giving motion to the whole body." See T. Hobbes, "Leviathan," in W. Molesworth, ed., *English Works* (London: Bohn, 1839), vol. 3, p. ix (originally written in 1651 by Hobbes). Another profound Galilean influence, discussed by Lowry, as cited, was his reliance on the Aristotelian principle of contiguity to explain the association of ideas, which was also picked up by Hobbes, Hartley, James Mill, and some of our modern learning theorists. See discussion by R. Lowry, *The Evolution of Psychological Theory: 1650 to the Present* (Chicago: Aldine, 1971).
11. Sambursky, as cited, p. 246.
12. For a good discussion of the physicalistic doctrine as it pertains to psychology, see K. V. Wilkes, *Physicalism: Studies in Philosophical Psychology* (Atlantic Highlands, N.J.: Humanities Press, 1978).
13. Lowry, *The Evolution of Psychological Theory*, as cited.
14. *Ibid.*
15. Sambursky, as cited, p. 303.
16. Lowry, as cited. Wilkes, as cited.
17. See I. Aleksander, *The Human Machine: A View of Intelligent Mechanisms* (St. Saphorin, Switzerland: Georgi, 1977).
18. D. Hume, *A Treatise of Human Nature: Being an Attempt to Introduce the Experimental Method of Reasoning into Moral Subjects* (London: Oxford University Press, 1978). See also discussion of Hume by A. B. Levison, *Knowledge and Society: An Introduction to the Philosophy of the Social Sciences* (New York: Bobbs-Merrill, 1974).
19. For portrayal of Hume as antirationalist, see discussion by K. Popper, *Objective Knowledge: An Evolutionary Approach* (Oxford: Clarendon, 1972), pp. 85f.
20. See J. Locke, *The Second Treatise of Government* (New York:

Liberal Arts Press, 1952). For example, he emphasized social order as a *law of nature* by which human rights and responsibilities are indisputably determined.

21. Hume, as cited, p. 128.

22. Popper, as cited, p. 4.

23. Hume, as cited, p. 148.

24. *Ibid.*, p. 76.

25. There were eight rules given by Hume; *ibid.*, pp. 173–175 for discussion.

26. D. Hume, *Inquiry Concerning Human Understanding* (New York: Liberal Arts Press, 1955), p. 24 (originally published 1748). See discussion by T. Mischel, "Scientific and Philosophical Psychology: A Historical Introduction," in T. Mischel, ed., *Human Action: Conceptual and Empirical Issues* (New York: Academic Press, 1969).

27. R. Calinger, "Kant and Newtonian Science: The Pre-Critical Period," *Isis*, 1979, vol. 70, pp. 349–362.

28. *Ibid.*

29. Kant wrote in 1755 in his *Allgemeine Naturgeschichte und Theorie des Himmels*: "Out of its universal dissolution and dissipation I see a beautiful and orderly whole quite naturally developing itself. This does not take place by accident, or by chance, but it is perceived that natural qualities bring it about. And are we not thereby moved to ask, why matter must just have had laws which aim at order and conformity? Was it possible that many things, each of which has its own nature independent of the others, should determine each other of themselves just in such a way that a well-ordered whole should arise therefore; and if they do this, is it not an origin at first, which must have been a universal Supreme Intelligence, in which the nature of things were devised for common combined purposes? . . . and there is a God, just because nature even in chaos cannot proceed otherwise than regularly and according to order." For longer excerpt, see Sambursky, as cited, p. 338.

30. Although Kant also subscribed to Newton's formulation, he nonetheless argued that the human intellect imposed its own laws on the sensual morass. Space is an innate organizing principle of the mind, Kant asserted. Gestalt psychology was later to seize on this idea, to maintain that space is not based on experience but is a pure intuition, a framework knitted together by nature and automatic association. See discussion by E. B. Newman, "Newton, Physics, and the Psychology of the Nineteenth Cen-

tury," *American Journal of Psychology,* 1969, vol. 82, pp. 400–406.

31. To be sure, Planck's concept of energy quanta went practically unrecognized even in the literature of physics for several years. See discussion by M. J. Klein, "Max Planck and the Beginnings of the Quantum Theory," *Archive for History of Exact Sciences,* 1962, vol. 1, pp. 459–479. Also pertinent, see B. Barber, "Resistance by Scientists to Scientific Discovery," *Science,* 1961, vol. 134, pp. 596–602.

32. Nineteenth-century physics had systematized the understanding of inorganic nature into mechanics, governed by Newtonian laws, and electricity, governed by Maxwell's equations, and there was an effort made to bridge these two. For discussion, see M. R. Cohen, *Reason and Nature: An Essay on the Meaning of Scientific Method* (New York: Dover, 1978), p. 231.

33. T. Verhave, "Psychologies of Women and Race in 19th Century England and the U.S.A.: The Use and Abuse of the Electric Metaphor," mimeod paper, undated, Queens College/City University of New York Department of Psychology.

34. From G. M. Beard, *Sexual Neurasthenia, Its Hygiene, Causes Symptoms, and Treatment: With a Chapter on Diet for the Nervous* (New York: Treat, 1884). Quoted in Verhave, as cited.

35. A. Comte, *Cours de Philosophie Positive* (London: Croom Helm, 1974). G. W. Allport mentions that Comte also asked himself how an individual could be both cause and consequence of society. At the end of his life Comte wrestled with a "true final science" designed to comprehend man as a product as well as a creative agent of society. For discussion, see G. W. Allport, "The Historical Background of Modern Social Psychology," in G. Lindzey and E. Aronson, eds., *The Handbook of Social Psychology* (Reading, Mass.: Addison-Wesley, 1968), vol. 1.

36. Lowry, "Galilean and Newtonian Influences on Psychological Thought," as cited.

37. William McDougall's model of psychology was even more overtly hydraulic, being replete with sluice gates, pipes, locks, and "bubbling over": W. McDougall, *An Outline of Psychology* (London: Methuen, 1923). For discussion of concept of mental energy as a mechanistic metaphor in psychoanalysis, see L. Henderson, "On Mental Energy," *British Journal of Psychology,* 1972, vol. 63, pp. 1–7; J. J. Putnam, "A Plea for the Study of Philosophic Methods in Preparation for Psychoanalytic Work," *Journal of Abnormal Psychology,* 1911, vol. 6, pp. 249–264; P. L.

Wachtel, "Psychology, Metapsychology, and Psychoanalysis," *Journal of Abnormal Psychology*, 1969, vol. 79, pp. 651–660.

38. E. G. Boring, *A History of Experimental Psychology* (New York: Appleton-Century-Crofts, 1957), p. 316.

39. K. Danziger, "The Positivist Repudiation of Wundt," *Journal of the History of the Behavioral Sciences*, 1979, vol. 15, pp. 205–230. K. Danziger, "Wundt and the Two Traditions of Psychology," in R. W. Rieber, ed., *Wilhelm Wundt and the Making of a Scientific Psychology* (New York: Plenum, 1980). R. M. Farr, "On Reading Darwin and Discovering Social Psychology," in R. Gilmour and S. Duck, eds., *The Development of Social Psychology* (London: Academic Press, 1980); R. M. Farr, "Homo Sociopsychologicus," in A. Chapman and D. Jones, eds., *Models of Man* (Leicester, England: British Psychological Society, 1980); A. L. Blumenthal, "The Founding Father We Never Knew," *Contemporary Psychology*, 1979, vol. 24, pp. 547–550. W. Wundt, "Folk Psychology: Language, Myth, and Custom," in W. S. Sahakian, ed., *Social Psychology: Experimentation, Theory, Research* (Scranton, Pa.: Intext, 1972). Also pertinent to this discussion, see D. E. Leary, "The Philosophical Development of the Conception of Psychology in Germany, 1780–1850," *Journal of the History of the Behavioral Sciences*, 1978, vol. 14, pp. 113–121; D. E. Leary, "Wundt and After: Psychology's Shifting Relations with the Natural Sciences, Social Sciences, and Philosophy," *Journal of the History of the Behavioral Sciences*, 1979, vol. 15, pp. 231–241.

40. Danziger, "The Positivist Repudiation of Wundt," as cited.

41. *Ibid.*

42. J. R. Royce, H. Coward, E. Egan, F. Kessel, and L. Mos, "Psychological Epistemology: A Critical Review of the Empirical Literature and the Theoretical Issues," *Genetic Psychology Monographs*, 1978, vol. 97, pp. 265–353.

43. Leary, "Wundt and After," as cited. Leary notes three German philosophers, in particular, who had evolved the naturalistic paradigm of psychology: J. F. Fries, J. F. Herbart, and F. E. Beneke—although at the same time, certain natural scientists, such as Helmholtz, were also open to the possibilities of such a paradigm in sensory psychology.

44. O. Külpe, *Outlines of Psychology* (New York: Macmillan, 1895), p. 4.

45. *Ibid.*, p. 12.

46. G. Lippmann, "A Vote for James: The 'First' Lab Debate Continues," *APA Monitor*, 1979, vol. 10, no. 5, p. 3.
47. C. G. Mueller, "Some Origins of Psychology as a Science," *Annual Review of Psychology*, 1979, vol. 30, pp. 9–29.
48. R. Evans, "Manual Labors: Titchener's Contribution," *APA Monitor*, 1979, vol. 10, no. 5, p. 3. See also M. Hale, Jr., *Human Science and Social Order* (Philadelphia, Pa.: Temple University Press, 1980).
49. P. W. Bridgman, *The Logic of Modern Physics* (New York: Macmillan, 1937). See discussion by E. R. Hilgard, "Controversies Over Consciousness and the Rise of Cognitive Psychology," *Australian Psychologist*, 1977, vol. 12, pp. 7–26; and symposium in *The Scientific Monthly*, October 1954 issue, especially articles by H. Margenau, G. Bergmann, C. G. Hempel, R. B. Lindsay, and Bridgman.
50. Sambursky, as cited, p. 506.
51. E. G. Boring, *The Physical Dimension of Consciousness* (New York: Century, 1933). Quoted from Danziger, "The Positivist Repudiation of Wundt," as cited, pp. 6, 8.
52. Mueller, as cited.
53. See M. W. Calkins, "A Reconciliation Between Structural and Functional Psychology," *Psychological Review*, 1906, vol. 13, p. 61 for contemporary definitions.
54. D. Cohen, *J. B. Watson, The Founder of Behaviorism: A Biography* (Boston, Mass.: Routledge and Kegan Paul, 1979).
55. J. B. Watson, "Psychology as the Behaviorist Views It," *Psychological Review*, 1913, vol. 20, pp. 158–177.
56. K. F. Muenzinger, "Physical and Psychological Reality," *Psychological Review*, 1927, vol. 34, pp. 220–233. See also discussion by B. D. Mackenzie, *Behaviorism and the Limits of Scientific Method* (Atlantic Highlands, N.J.: Humanities Press, 1977).
57. See, for example, A. P. Weiss, "Behaviorism and Behavior, I," *Psychological Review*, 1924, vol. 31, pp. 32f.
58. See discussions by H. Haines and G. M. Vaughn, "Was 1898, a 'Great Date' in the History of Experimental Social Psychology?" *Journal of the History of the Behavioral Sciences*, 1979, vol. 15, pp. 323–332; J. Morawksi, "Early Views of Social Psychology's Progress: Some Comments on the Past and Current Functions of Historical Scholarship," Unpublished paper, Carleton University Department of Psychology, 1979.
59. Haines and Vaughn, as cited.

60. N. Triplett, "The Dynamogenic Factors in Pacemaking and Competition," *American Journal of Psychology*, 1898, vol. 9, pp. 507–533. Triplett's paper was published in volume 9 which included the years 1897 and 1898. For implications, see Haines and Vaughn, as cited, especially footnote 4 of their article.

61. S. Tunis, "Norman Triplett: Father of Experimental Social Psychology," *SASP Newsletter*, February 1980.

62. J. Dewey, "The Need for Social Psychology," *Psychological Review*, 1917, vol. 24, pp. 266–277. See also discussion by Leary, "Wundt and After," as cited, p. 237.

63. A. P. Weiss, "A Set of Postulates for Social Psychology," *Journal of Abnormal and Social Psychology*, 1926, vol. 21, pp. 203–211.

64. C. Murchison, ed., *A Handbook of Social Psychology* (Worcester, Mass.: Clark University Press, 1935).

65. G. Murphy and L. B. Murphy, *Experimental Social Psychology* (New York: Harper, 1931).

66. D. Cartwright, "Contemporary Social Psychology in Historical Perspective," *Social Psychology Quarterly*, 1979, vol. 42, pp. 82–93.

67. *Ibid.*, p. 84.

68. See discussion by W. J. McGuire, "The Nature of Attitudes and Attiude Change," in G. Lindzey and E. Aronson, eds., *The Handbook of Social Psychology* (Reading, Mass.: Addison-Wesley, 1969).

69. Hull's theoretical research was replete with citations to Hovland's early laboratory work. See C. L. Hull, *Principles of Behavior* (New York: Appleton-Century-Crofts, 1943).

70. Best known was the research on communication at Yale University under Hovland's direction; see the following: C. I. Hovland, I. L. Janis, and H. H. Kelley, *Communication and Persuasion: Psychological Studies of Opinion Change* (New Haven, Conn.: Yale University Press, 1953); C. I. Hovland et al., *The Order of Presentation in Persuasion* (New Haven, Conn.: Yale University Press, 1957); I. L. Janis et al., *Personality and Persuasibility* (New Haven, Conn.: Yale University Press, 1959); M. J. Rosenberg et al., *Attitude Organization and Change: An Analysis of Consistency Among Attitude Components* (New Haven, Conn.: Yale University Press, 1960); M. Sherif and C. I. Hovland, *Social Judgment: Assimilation and Contrast Effects in Communication and Attitude Change* (New Haven, Conn.: Yale University Press, 1961).

71. K. Lewin, The Principles of Topological Psychology (New York: McGraw-Hill, 1936).

72. For critiques, see: O. L. Reiser, "Aristotelian, Galilean and Non-Aristotelian Modes of Thinking," Psychological Review, 1939, vol. 46, pp. 151–162; J. R. Kantor, "Concerning Physical Analogies in Psychology," American Journal of Psychology, 1936, vol. 48, pp. 153–164. An alternative view appears in M. A. Lewin, "Kurt Lewin's View of Social Psychology: The Crisis of 1977 and the Crisis of 1927," Personality and Social Psychology Bulletin, 1977, vol. 3, pp. 159–172.

73. Gestalt psychology had concentrated on a static organization of processes; Lewin stressed the topological structure of a situation in a person's life and asserted that behavior "depends only upon the psychological field at that time." Quoted from K. Lewin, "Defining the 'Field' at a Given Time," Psychological Review, 1943, vol. 50, pp. 292–310, especially p. 294. See also discussion in K. Lewin, A Dynamic Theory of Personality: Selected Papers (New York: McGraw-Hill, 1935). For other critiques during this period, see: C. E. Spearman, "The Confusion That is Gestalt-Psychology," American Journal of Psychology, 1937, vol. 50, pp. 369–383; H. E. Garrett, "Lewin's 'Topological' Psychology: An Evaluation," Psychological Review, 1939, vol. 46, pp. 517–524; I.D. London, "Psychologists' Misuse of the Auxiliary Concepts of Physics and Mathematics," Psychological Review, 1944, vol. 51, pp. 266–291.

74. K. L. Higbee and M. G. Wells, "Some Research Trends in Social Psychology in the 1960s," American Psychologist, 1972, vol. 27, pp. 963–966. See also R. Christie, "Some Implications of Research Trends in Social Psychology," in O. Klineberg and R. Christie, eds., Perspectives in Social Psychology (New York: Holt, Rinehart & Winston, 1965).

75. E. P. Hollander, "The Society of Experimental Social Psychology: An Historical Note," Journal of Personality and Social Psychology, 1968, vol. 9, pp. 280–282.

76. E. C. Sanford, "Psychology and Physics," Psychological Review, 1903, vol. 10, pp. 105–119, especially p. 106. This was Sanford's presidential address of December 1902. His notion of an anthropomorphic model of man is perhaps reminiscent of the recent theoretical model articulated by R. Harré and P. F. Secord in The Explanation of Social Behaviour (Oxford: Blackwell, 1972). Their recommendations for dealing with the various problems en-

gendered by the experimentalism lead them to argue for an eth-
nogenic orientation with emphasis on the rules that human beings follow within specific circumstances.
77. L. L. Bernard, "On the Making of Textbooks in Social Psychology," *Journal of Educational Psychology*, 1931, vol. 5, pp. 67–81.
78. Allport, as cited. In his early work, Hovland had likened the process of attitude change to the learning of a habit or skill, but by
the late 1950s he, too, had begun to realize that laboratory studies were not exact analogies of field studies due to uncontrolled
confounding variables in the laboratory. See C. I. Hovland, "Re-
conciling Conflicting Results Derived from Experimental and
Survey Studies of Attitude Change," *American Psychologist*,
1959, vol. 14, pp. 8–17.

3   The Artifact Crisis

1. For longer excerpt from *Dialogo*, see anthology edited by S. Sambursky, *Physical Thought: From the Presocratics to the Quantum
Physicists: An Anthology* (New York: Pica Press, 1975), p. 217.
2. For discussion of the human subject's changing role in psychology's history, see: D. P. Schultz, "The Human Subject in Psychological Research," *Psychological Bulletin*, 1969, vol. 72, pp.
214–228; J. G. Adair, *The Human Subject: The Social Psychology
of the Psychological Experiment* (Boston: Little, Brown, 1973).
3. I. Silverman, "Artifactual Behavior of Subjects in Attitude Change
Studies," Paper presented in symposium on "Methodological
Problems and Research in Social Influence," Southeastern Psychological Association meeting, February 1969.
4. O. Pfungst, *Clever Hans (The Horse of Mr. von Osten)*, edited
with an introduction by R. Rosenthal (New York: Holt, Rinehart
& Winston, 1965) (first published by Henry Holt & Co., 1911).
5. F. J. Roethlisberger and W. J. Dickson, *Management and the
Worker* (Cambridge, Mass.: Harvard University Press, 1939).
6. See discussions by A. Carey, "The Hawthorne Studies: A Radical
Criticism," *American Sociological Review*, 1967, vol. 32, pp.
403–416; D. Miller and W. Form, *Industrial Sociology* (New
York: Harper, 1951).
7. See R. Sommer, "Hawthorne Dogma," *Psychological Bulletin*,
1968, vol. 70, pp. 592–595.
8. But the nature of these effects is uncertain; there can be a positive change in behavior, as the researchers in the Hawthorne
study observed, or even a negative change as others have re-

ported. See R. L. Dipboye and M. F. Flanagan, "Research Findings in the Field More Generalizable Than in the Laboratory?" *American Psychologist,* 1979, vol. 34, pp. 141–150; V. E. O'Leary, "The Hawthorne Effect in Reverse: Trainee Orientation for the Hard-Core Unemployed Woman," *Journal of Applied Psychology,* 1972, vol. 56, pp. 491–494.

9. S. Rosenzweig, "The Experimental Situation as a Psychological Problem," *Psychological Review,* 1933, vol. 40, pp. 337–354.

10. *Ibid.,* p. 337.

11. See also L. J. Stricker, "The True Deceiver," *Psychological Bulletin,* 1967, vol. 68, pp. 13–20.

12. R. Rosenthal, *Experimenter Effects in Behavioral Research* (New York: Appleton-Century-Crofts, 1966). Enlarged edition published by Irvington Publishers, Halsted Press Division of Wiley, 1976.

13. For an example outside of psychology, see S. J. Gould, "Morton's Ranking of Races by Cranial Capacity," *Science,* 1978, vol. 200, pp. 503–509.

14. J. J. Sherwood and M. Nataupsky, "Predicting the Conclusions of Negro-White Intelligence Research from Biographical Characteristics of the Investigator," *Journal of Personality and Social Psychology,* 1968, vol. 8, pp. 53–58.

15. In a similar vein, Michael Mahoney has found that conclusions reached about the scientific value of research articles tend to be strongly biased against manuscripts that report results contrary to the referee's theoretical perspective. For discussions see: M. J. Mahoney, "Publication Prejudices: An Experimental Study of Confirmatory Bias in the Peer Review System," *Cognitive Therapy and Research,* 1977, vol. 1, pp. 161–175; M. J. Mahoney, *Scientist As Subject: The Psychological Imperative* (Cambridge, Mass.: Ballinger, 1976).

16. A famous example that has been popularized by the media was that of the biologist Paul Kammerer, who was engaged in research on the Lamarkian hypothesis of the inheritance of acquired characteristics. Kammerer spent most of his adult life trying experimentally to demonstrate that skills and improvements in physique acquired by one generation of animals are to some extent inherited by their offspring. This Lamarkian view, which regards evolution as the cumulative effect of the virtues of successive generations, can be contrasted with the Darwinian view of evolution which emphasizes blind chance and selective pressures. All that remained of Kammerer's experimental animals

after World War I was one lone preserved specimen of a toad with a black thumb pad purportedly acquired through Lamarkian evolution. But a suspicious investigator found that the blackened thumb pad had been tampered with. The visible coloration had been produced by India ink, not by pigmentation. A few weeks after this disclosure, his reputation ruined, Kammerer shot himself. To this day it cannot be said with certainty whether the forgery was committed by Kammerer or by a different person without his knowledge. An account of this case can be found in A. Koestler, *The Case of the Midwife Toad* (New York: Random House, 1972). See also D. Weinstein, "Fraud in Science," *Social Science Quarterly*, 1979, vol. 59, pp. 639–652.

17. N. Wade, "IQ and Heredity: Suspicion of Fraud Beclouds Classic Experiment," *Science*, 1976, vol. 194, pp. 916–919. L. S. Hearnshaw, *Cyril Burt, Psychologist* (Ithaca, N.Y.: Cornell University Press, 1979). D. D. Dorfman, "The Cyril Burt Question: New Findings," *Science*, 1978, vol. 201, pp. 1177–1186.

18. L. Kamin, *The Science and Politics of IQ* (Potomac, Md.:. Erlbaum, 1974).

19. O. Gillie, "Burt's Missing Ladies," *Science*, 1979, vol. 204, pp. 1035–1039. For a discussion of entire incident, see also O. Gillie, "Sir Cyril Burt and the Great IQ Fraud," *New Statesman*, November 24, 1978.

20. For example, see: A. R. Jensen, "Sir Cyril Burt in Perspective," *American Psychologist*, 1978, vol. 33, pp. 499–503; M. McAskie, "Carelessness or Fraud in Sir Cyril Burt's Kinship Data?: A Critique of Jensen's Analysis," *American Psychologist*, 1978, vol. 33, pp. 496–498; D. Cohen, "British Society Takes Stand on Burt; Tackles Practical Problems," *APA Monitor*, 1980, vol. 11, no. 5, pp. 1, 9.

21. R. Rosenthal, "Biasing Effects of Experimenters," *Et Cetera: A Review of General Semantics*, 1977, vol. 34, pp. 253–264. Also see D. K. Rumenik, D. R. Capasso, and C. Hendrick, "Experimenter Sex Effects in Behavioral Research," *Psychological Bulletin*, 1977, vol. 84, pp. 852–877.

22. Rosenthal, "Biasing Effects of Experimenters," as cited.

23. H. B. Hovey, "Effects of General Distraction on the Higher Thought Processes," *American Journal of Psychology*, 1928, vol. 40, pp. 585–591. See discussion also in Sommer, as cited.

24. R. K. Merton, "The Self-Fulfilling Prophecy," *Antioch Review*, 1948, vol. 8, pp. 193–210.

25. Michael Martin argues that the Rosenthal effect is disanalogous

with a self-fulfilling prophecy and instead is more like a "reference prediction" as defined by R. Buck. For discussion of this point, see M. Martin, "The Philosophical Importance of the Rosenthal Effect," *Journal for the Theory of Social Behaviour*, 1977, vol. 7, pp. 81–97; R. C. Buck, "Reflexive Prediction," *Philosophy of Science*, 1964, vol. 30, pp. 359–369.

26. R. Rosenthal, *An Attempt at the Experimental Induction of the Defense Mechanism of Projection*, unpublished doctoral dissertation, University of California, Los Angeles, 1956.

27. S. Freud, *Collected Papers* (London: Hogarth, 1953), vol. 4, p. 78.

28. See, for example, T. X. Barber and M. J. Silver, "Fact, Fiction, and the Experimenter Bias Effect," *Psychological Bulletin Monograph Supplement*, 1968, vol. 70, pp. 1–29; R. Rosenthal, "Experimenter Expectancy and the Reassuring Nature of the Null Hypothesis Decision Procedure," *Psychological Bulletin Monograph Supplement*, 1968, vol. 70, pp. 30–47.

29. R. Rosenthal and R. Lawson, "A Longitudinal Study of the Effects of Experimenter Bias on the Operant Learning of Laboratory Rats," *Journal of Psychiatric Research*, 1964, vol. 2, pp. 61–72.

30. See, for example, M. L. Shames, "On the Metamethodological Dimension of the 'Expectancy Paradox,' " *Philosophy of Science*, 1979, vol. 46, pp. 383–388.

31. See R. Rosenthal and D. B. Rubin, "Interpersonal Expectancy Effect," *Behavioral and Brain Sciences*, 1978, vol. 1, pp. 377–386.

32. Rosenthal, *Experimenter Effects in Behavioral Research*, as cited.

33. See discussions by N. Friedman, *The Social Nature of Psychological Research: The Psychological Experiment as a Social Interaction* (New York: Basic Books, 1967); R. A. Jones and J. Cooper, "Mediation of Experimenter Effects," *Journal of Personality and Social Psychology*, 1971, vol. 20, pp. 70–74.

34. Martin, as cited.

35. J. Converse, "On Dealing with the Expectations of Social Scientists: The Dialectic of Faith and Objectivity," unpublished paper, Temple University Department of Psychology, January 1980.

36. See, for example, M. T. Orne and K. E. Scheibe, "The Contribution of Nondeprivation Factors in the Production of Sensory Deprivation Effects: The Psychology of the 'Panic Button'," *Journal of Abnormal and Social Psychology*, 1964, vol. 68, pp. 3–12; L. A. Gustafson and M. T. Orne, "Effects of Perceived Role and Role Success on the Detection of Deception," *Journal of Applied Psychology*, 1965, vol. 49, pp. 412–417; M. T. Orne and F. J. Evans, "Inadvertent Termination of Hypnosis with Hypnotized

and Simulating Subjects," *International Journal of Clinical and Experimental Hypnosis*, 1966, vol. 14, pp. 61–78.

37. M. T. Orne, "Hypnosis, Motivation, and the Ecological Validity of the Psychological Experiment," in W. J. Arnold and M. M. Page, eds., *Nebraska Symposium on Motivation* (Lincoln: University of Nebraska Press, 1970), especially pp. 194f.

38. M. T. Orne, "The Nature of Hypnosis: Artifact and Essence," *Journal of Abnormal and Social Psychology*, 1959, vol. 58, pp. 277–299.

39. M. T. Orne, "On the Social Psychology of the Psychological Experiment: With Particular Reference to Demand Characteristics and Their Implications," *American Psychologist*, 1962, vol. 17, pp. 776–783.

40. I. Silverman, "Motives Underlying the Behavior of the Subject in the Psychological Experiment," paper presented at American Psychological Association meeting, Chicago, September 1965.

41. M. J. Rosenberg, "The Conditions and Consequences of Evaluation Apprehension," in R. Rosenthal and R. L. Rosnow, eds., *Artifact in Behavioral Research* (New York: Academic Press, 1969). In contrast to Orne's conception of the subject who cooperates to help science and in doing so "looks good," Rosenberg argued that the subject cooperates *only in order* to look good; thus Rosenberg's subject is egoistic in orientation, while Orne's is ostensibly altruistic. This still might not seem like a crucial theoretical distinction, for it is plausible that culture and circumstances may determine which of these motives will prevail in a given instance. Experiments that have sought to pit the two motives against each other have found that there is usually a tendency for the subjects to try to project a favorable image even if this means not acceding to demand characteristics. Imagine a conflict situation in which the research subject had to choose between responding in accordance with the experimenter's hypotheses as opposed to the subject's own wish to appear intelligent. Suppose further that uncertainty and anxiety which gave rise to rumors and campus scuttlebutt led the subject to believe that acceding to the experimenter's hypotheses would make the subject seem gullible and thus appear stupid in the experimenter's eyes. In this situation Rosenberg's prediction seems to prevail over Orne's—that is, the subject would rather look good than help the experimenter or the cause of science, if the subject thinks that helping the experimenter will cause him to evaluate the subject unfavorably. For discussion of this effect and experimental evi-

dence bearing on it, see R. L. Rosnow, B. E. Goodstadt, J. M. Suls, and A. G. Gitter, "More on the Social Psychology of the Experiment: When Compliance Turns to Self-Defense," *Journal of Personality and Social Psychology*, 1973, vol. 27, pp. 337–343. But for an alternative position, see B. Spinner, *Subject Behaviour in the Laboratory: Objective Self-Awareness or Evaluation Apprehension*, Doctoral dissertation, University of Manitoba Psychology Department, 1979.

42. L. Festinger, *A Theory of Cognitive Dissonance* (Stanford, Cal.: Stanford University Press, 1957).

43. See, for example, W. J. McGuire, "Attitudes and Opinions," *Annual Review of Psychology*, 1966, vol. 17, pp. 475–514; K. E. Weick, "When Prophecy Pales: The Fate of Dissonance Theory," *Psychological Reports*, 1965, vol. 16, pp. 1261–1275; N. P. Chapanis and A. Chapanis, "Cognitive Dissonance: Five Years Later," *Psychological Bulletin*, 1964, vol. 61, pp. 1–22; I. Silverman, "In Defense of Dissonance Theory: Reply to Chapanis and Chapanis," *Psychological Bulletin*, 1964, vol. 62, pp. 205–209.

44. M. J. Rosenberg, "When Dissonance Fails: On Eliminating Evaluation Apprehension From Attitude Measurement," *Journal of Personality and Social Psychology*, 1965, vol. 1, pp. 28–42. Several attempts were made to reconcile Rosenberg's findings with those of dissonance theory; see, for example, J. M. Carlsmith, B. E. Collins, and R. L. Helmreich, "Studies in Forced Compliance: I. The Effect of Pressure for Compliance on Attitude Change Produced by Face-to-Face Role Playing and Anonymous Essay Writing," *Journal of Personality and Social Psychology*, 1966, vol. 4, pp. 1–13.

45. It was possible to imagine a number of control procedures for coping with each interactional artifact one at a time. But trying to devise workable procedures for differentiating each effect was proving to be a more difficult task. See, for example, S. J. Weber and T. D. Cook, "Subject Effects in Laboratory Research: An Examination of Subject Roles, Demand Characteristics, and Valid Inference," *Psychological Bulletin*, 1972, vol. 77, pp. 273–295. One possibility was to control or circumvent many of these artifacts all at one time, by using field experiments, simulations, etc. Another possibility was to try to specify their mediating properties and then control for them in some way. In my own theoretical research, I tried to show how these artifacts correlated to a few intervening variables that could be dealt with by the use of simple procedures, theoretically derived. See R. L. Rosnow

and L. S. Aiken, "Mediation of Artifacts in Behavioral Research," *Journal of Experimental Social Psychology*, 1973, vol. 9, pp. 181–201; R. L. Rosnow and D. J. Davis, "Demand Characteristics and the Psychological Experiment," *Et Cetera: A Review of General Semantics*, 1977, vol. 34, pp. 301–313.

Some social psychologists advocated role playing as an alternative to deception, and for a while there was a flurry of activity concerning this possibility. But the apparent weaknesses of role playing eventually mitigated against its acceptance except as a kind of quasi-control procedure. See discussion by A. G. Miller, "Role Playing: An Alternative to Deception," *American Psychologist*, 1972, vol. 27, pp. 623–636. Other pertinent references along these lines include the following: I. Silverman and A. D. Shulman, "A Conceptual Model of Artifact in Attitude Change Studies," *Sociometry*, 1970, vol. 33, pp. 97–107; D. T. Campbell, "Prospective: Artifact and Control," in R. Rosenthal and R. L. Rosnow, eds., *Artifact in Behavioral Research*, as cited; D. J. Bem and C. G. Lord, "Template Matching: A Proposal for Probing the Ecological Validity of Experimental Settings in Social Psychology," *Journal of Personality and Social Psychology*, 1979, vol. 37, pp. 833–846, especially p. 841.

4 The Ethics Crisis

1. See discussion by I. Silverman, "Crisis in Social Psychology: The Relevance of Relevance," *American Psychologist*, 1971, vol. 26, pp. 583–584.

2. L. J. Stricker, "The True Deceiver," *Psychological Bulletin*, 1967, vol. 68, pp. 13–20.

3. R. J. Menges, "Openness and Honesty Versus Coercion and Deception in Psychological Research," *American Psychologist*, 1973, vol. 28, pp. 1030–1034.

4. I. Silverman, A. D. Shulman, and D. L. Wiesenthal, "Effects of Deceiving and Debriefing Psychological Subjects on Performance in Later Experiments," *Journal of Personality and Social Psychology*, 1970, vol. 14, pp. 203–212.

5. In 1966, a book had been published by E. J. Webb, D. T. Campbell, R. D. Schwartz, and L. Sechrest, *Unobtrusive Measures: Nonreactive Research in the Social Sciences* (Chicago: Rand McNally), which was a veritable encyclopedia of hidden and disguised measurements of the dependent variable.

6. L. Humphreys, "New Styles in Homosexual Manliness," *Trans-Action*, 1971, vol. 8, pp. 38–46. L. Humphreys, *Tearoom Trade:*

Impersonal Sex in Public Places, second edition (Chicago: Aldine, 1975).

7. L. Humphreys, Letter in *Science* magazine, 1980, vol. 207, p. 714.

8. See discussion by P. D. Reynold, "Value Dilemmas in the Professional Conduct of Social Science," *International Social Science Journal,* 1975, vol. 27, pp. 563–611.

9. J. M. Darley, "The Importance of Being Earnest—and Ethical," *Contemporary Psychology,* 1980, vol. 25, pp. 14–15.

10. W. E. Vinacke, "Deceiving Experimental Subjects," *American Psychologist,* 1954, vol. 9, p. 155.

11. S. Milgram, *Obedience to Authority: An Experimental View* (New York: Harper & Row, 1974).

12. *Ibid.,* pp. 188–189.

13. H. Arendt, *Eichmann in Jerusalem: A Report on the Banality of Evil* (New York: Viking, 1963).

14. D. Baumrind, "Some Thoughts on Ethics of Research: After Reading Milgram's 'Behavioral Study of Obedience'," *American Psychologist,* 1964, vol. 19, pp. 421–423.

15. S. Milgram, "Behavioral Study of Obedience," *Journal of Abnormal and Social Psychology,* 1963, vol. 67, pp. 371–378, quoted from p. 377.

16. *Ibid.,* p. 375.

17. S. Milgram, "Issues in the Study of Obedience: A Reply to Baumrind," *American Psychologist,* 1964, vol. 19, pp. 848–852.

18. *Ibid.*

19. For discussion of this assertion, see, for example, S. D. Ross, *Moral Decision: An Introduction* (San Francisco: Freeman, Cooper, 1972), pp. 51f.

20. See L. Bickman and M. Zarantonello, "The Effects of Deception and Level of Obedience on Subjects' Ratings of the Milgram Study," *Personality and Social Psychology Bulletin,* 1978, vol. 4, pp. 81–85. In this study, adults were presented with four versions of Milgram's experimental design, in which both the degree of obedience and the amount of deception were varied in the descriptions. Those who read the versions indicating that a high level of obedience had resulted rated the design as potentially more harmful than those who read the versions indicating that a low level of obedience had resulted. These data suggest that perceptions of the Milgram experiments were possibly more contingent upon the outcome than upon the particular deception procedures used by him.

21. E. Brunswik, *Systematic and Representative Design of Psycho-*

logical Experiments With Results in Physical and Social Perception (Berkeley: University of California Press, 1957). Syllabus series no. 304.

22. Baumrind, as cited, p. 421. Rosenzweig had argued along similar lines in his 1933 article (see discussion in previous chapter), and Rosenberg would echo this theme in 1965 when he experimentally attacked a central proposition of Festinger's research on cognitive dissonance.

23. Baumrind, as cited, p. 421.

24. M. T. Orne and F. J. Evans, "Social Control in the Psychological Experiment: Antisocial Behavior and Hypnosis," Journal of Personality and Social Psychology, 1965, vol. 1, pp. 189–200.

25. M. T. Orne and C. H. Holland, "On the Ecological Validity of Laboratory Deceptions," International Journal of Psychiatry, 1968, vol. 6, pp. 282–293. For Milgram's reply, see S. Milgram, "Interpreting Obedience: Error and Evidence: A Reply to Orne and Holland," in A. G. Miller, ed., The Social Psychology of Psychological Research (New York: Free Press, 1972).

26. See, for example, J. Seeman, "Deception in Psychological Research," American Psychologist, 1969, vol. 24, pp. 1025–1028; L. Beckman and B. R. Bishop, "Deception in Psychological Research: A Reply to Seeman," American Psychologist, 1970, vol. 25, pp. 878–880.

27. H. C. Kelman, A Time to Speak: On Human Values and Social Research (San Francisco: Jossey-Bass, 1968), p. 211.

28. See, for example, H. K. Beecher, "Documenting the Abuses," Saturday Review, July 2, 1966, pp. 45–46; H. K. Beecher, Research and the Individual (Boston: Little Brown, 1970); J. Katz, Experimentation With Human Beings (New York: Russell Sage, 1972). For a more recent overview of moral concerns and scientific issues, see S. Bok, Lying: Moral Choice in Public and Private Life (New York: Pantheon, 1978).

29. See discussion by Kelman, as cited, pp. 202f.

30. See S. E. Asch, "Effects of Group Pressure Upon the Modification and Distortion of Judgments," in H. Guetzkow, ed., Groups, Leadership and Men (Pittsburgh, Pa.: Carnegie Press, 1951; and discussions by Silverman, as cited, especially p. 584; G. I. Schulman, "Asch Conformity Studies: Conformity to the Experimenter and/or to the Group," Sociometry, 1967, vol. 30, pp. 26–40.

31. See, for example, discussion by Z. Rubin, "Jokers Wild in the Lab," in J. B. Maas, ed., Readings in Psychology Today, third edition (Del Mar, Cal.: CRM Books, 1974).

32. Discussion by R. Rosenthal and R. L. Rosnow, *Primer of Methods for the Behavioral Sciences* (New York: Wiley, 1975), pp. 97f.
33. Bok, as cited, p. 199. Recent survey findings reveal that psychologists may hold views that are more ethically stringent than those given by their most typical human subjects; see D. S. Sullivan and T. E. Deiker, "Subject-Experimenter Perceptions of Ethical Issues in Human Research," *American Psychologist*, 1973, vol. 28, pp. 587–591.
34. For pertinent discussion, see J. Margolis, *Values and Conduct* (Oxford, England: Clarendon, 1971); B. C. Birchall, "Moral Life as the Obstacle to the Development of Ethical Theory," *Inquiry*, 1978, vol. 21, pp. 409–424. An interesting study that is also relevant is that by B. R. Schlenker and D. R. Forsyth, "On the Ethics of Psychological Research," *Journal of Experimental Social Psychology*, 1977, vol. 13, pp. 369–396.
35. See R. Sasson and T. M. Nelson, "The Human Experimental Subject in Context," *Canadian Psychologist*, 1969, vol. 10, pp. 409–437, especially pp. 423f.
36. W. Liemohn, "Research Involving Human Subjects," *Research Quarterly*, 1979, vol. 50, pp. 157–163. Also see Appendix I in "New Dimensions in Legal and Ethical Concepts for Human Research," *Annals of the New York Academy of Sciences*, vol. 169, pp. 590–591.
37. The final version appeared in *American Psychologist*, January 1973 issue. Preliminary drafts of this code were developed by S. W. Cook, G. A. Kimble, L. H. Hicks, W. J. McGuire, P. H. Schoggen, and M. B. Smith, and published in the *APA Monitor*; see 1971, vol. 2, no. 7, pp. 9–28 and 1972, vol. 3, pp. i–xix.
38. Reynold, as cited.
39. *Ibid.*
40. For general discussions, see the following: D. Baumrind, "Principles of Ethical Conduct in the Treatment of Subjects: Reaction to the Draft Report of the Committee on Ethical Standards in Psychological Research," *American Psychologist*, 1971, vol. 26, pp. 887–896; D. Baumrind, "Reactions to the May 1972 Draft Report of the Ad Hoc Committee on Ethical Standards in Psychological Research," *American Psychologist*, 1972, vol. 27, pp. 1083–1086; R. V. Alumbaugh, "Another 'Malleus Maleficarum,' " *American Psychologist*, 1972, vol. 27, pp. 897–899; F. N. Kerlinger, "Draft Report of the APA Committee on Ethical Standards in Psychological Research: A Critical Reaction," *American Psychologist*, 1972, vol. 27, pp. 894–896; W. W. May, "On Baumrind's Four

Commandments," *American Psychologist*, 1972, vol. 27, pp. 896–897; K. J. Gergen, "The Codification of Research Ethics: Views of a Doubting Thomas," *American Psychologist*, 1973, vol. 28, pp. 907–912.

41. J. H. Resnick and T. Schwartz, "Ethical Standards as an Independent Variable in Psychological Research," *American Psychologist*, 1973, vol. 28, pp. 134–139.
42. See H. C. Kelman, "The Rights of the Subject in Social Research: An Analysis in Terms of Relative Power and Legitimacy," *American Psychologist*, 1972, vol. 27, pp. 989–1016.
43. C. Argyris, "Some Unintended Consequences of Rigorous Research," *Psychological Bulletin*, 1968, vol. 70, pp. 185–197.
44. *Ibid.*, p. 189.
45. For discussion, see K. L. Higbee and M. G. Wells, "Some Research Trends in Social Psychology During the 1960s," *American Psychologist*, 1972, vol. 27, pp. 963–966; J. Jung, "Current Practices and Problems in the Use of College Students for Psychological Research," *Canadian Psychologist*, 1969, vol. 10, pp. 280–290; D. P. Schultz, "The Human Subject in Psychological Research," *Psychological Bulletin*, 1969, vol. 72, pp. 214–228; R. G. Smart, "Subject Selection Bias in Psychological Research," *Canadian Psychologist*, 1966, vol. 7a, pp. 115–121.
46. Q. McNemar, "Opinion-Attitude Methodology," *Psychological Bulletin*, 1946, vol. 43, pp. 289–374.
47. R. Rosenthal and R. L. Rosnow, *The Volunteer Subject* (New York: Wiley-Interscience, 1975). For a summary, see R. L. Rosnow and R. Rosenthal, "The Volunteer Subject Revisited," *Australian Journal of Psychology*, 1976, vol. 28, pp. 97–108.
48. Volunteer bias is also recognized as a problem in experimental economics, in clinical therapeutic evaluations, and other areas: See, for example, J. H. Kagel, R. C. Battalio, and J. M. Walker, "Volunteer Artifacts in Experiments in Economics: Specification of the Problem and Some Initial Data From a Small Scale Field Experiment," in V. L. Smith, ed., *Research in Experimental Economics* (Greenwich, Conn.: JAI Press, 1979); M. L. MacDonald, "Social Psychology of Psychologists: Volunteer Vs. Nonvolunteer Therapists," *Psychological Reports*, 1979, vol. 44, pp. 311–314. But for a difference of opinion, see A. W. Kruglanski, "Much Ado About the 'Volunteer Artifacts,' " *Journal of Personality and Social Psychology*, 1973, vol. 28, pp. 348–354; and reply by R. L. Rosnow and R. Rosenthal, "Taming of the Volunteer Problem: On Coping With Artifacts By Benign Neglect," *Journal of Personality and Social Psychology*, 1974, vol. 30, pp. 188–190.

49. B. H. Gray, R. A. Cooke, and A. S. Tannenbaum, "Research Involving Human Subjects," *Science,* 1978, vol. 201, pp. 1094–1101.

50. R. J. Smith, "Electroshock Experiment at Albany Violates Ethics Guidelines," *Science,* 1977, vol. 198, pp. 383–386; J. T. Tedeschi and G. G. Gallup, Jr., "Human Subjects Research," *Science,* 1977, vol. 198, pp. 1099–1100. See reply to Tedeschi and Gallup, *ibid.,* p. 1100, same issue.

51. For discussion, see A. J. Kimmel, "Ethics and Human Subjects Research: A Delicate Balance," *American Psychologist,* 1979, vol. 34, pp. 633–635.

5 The Relevance Crisis

1. J. Morawski, "Early Views of Social Psychology's Progress: Some Comments on the Past and Current Functions of Historical Scholarship," unpublished paper, Carleton University Department of Psychology, 1979.

2. Morawski quotes a conclusion to a 1927 social psychology textbook: "The admitted lack of scientific rigor and definite organization of social psychology is due to its youth. Every science as it seeks to contribute to the needs of men must first be regarded as founded in such needs. As it seeks to find reliability for its offerings, it must perforce resort to the method of experimentation, and in so doing it must acquire, analyze, and classify facts. Then such a science may attempt to formulate its laws, which in turn afford a basis for the prediction and control of social events." Quoted from J. W. Sprowls, *Social Psychology Interpreted* (Baltimore, Md.: Williams & Wilkens, 1927, p. 252.

3. Pertinent to this point are the following: See I. Silverman, "Why Social Psychology Fails," *Canadian Psychological Review,* 1977, vol. 18, pp. 353–358; C. Krauthammer, "The Expanding Shrink," *The New Republic,* 1979, September 22, pp. 10–12.

4. Many of psychology's early leaders also were motivated by social concerns, which led them to focus on particular theoretical issues and social problems for investigation. Indeed, the plea for an action-oriented social science was voiced throughout the latter half of the nineteenth century, motivated apparently by political uprisings in Europe that sparked concerns for dealing with social issues. The British National Association for the Promotion of the Social Sciences was founded in 1857, and the Association Internationale pour le Progres des Sciences, modeled after the British Association, was begun five years later by a group of

prominent Belgian citizens. For discussion, see D. Leary, "A Century of Social Concern," *APA Monitor*, 1979, vol. 10, no. 6, p. 3; E. Apfelbaum, "Some Overlooked Early European Social Psychologies," paper presented at symposium on "Historical Perspectives on Social Psychology," at American Psychological Association meeting, New York City, September 3, 1979.

5. There was a crisis of experimentalism in the 1920s resulting from such a cleavage. E. B. Titchener, Wundt's student, had created the Society of Experimentalists in the conviction that the American Psychological Association as a pluralistic organization could not represent the scientific ideal. At the meeting of the Experimentalists in 1917, a discussion ensued concerning how psychologists could assist the war effort. During the 1920s the seed planted at that meeting grew into what many basic researchers saw as a pernicious tendency toward applied psychology after World War I. For discussion, see J. M. O'Donnell, "The Crisis of Experimentalism in the 1920s: E. G. Boring and His Uses of History," *American Psychologist*, 1979, vol. 34, pp. 289–295.

6. Leary, as cited.

7. R. S. Lynd, *Knowledge for What? The Place of Social Science in American Culture* (Princeton, N.J.: Princeton University Press, 1939), pp. 2–3.

8. D. Cartwright, "Social Psychology in the United States During the Second World War," *Human Relations*, 1948, vol. 1, pp. 333–352.

9. For examples, see C. I. Hovland, A. A. Lumsdaine, and F. D. Sheffield, *Experiments on Mass Communication* (Princeton, N.J.: Princeton University Press, 1949).

10. For recent discussions, see M. L. Papanek, "Kurt Lewin and His Contributions to Modern Management Theory," *Academy of Management Proceedings*, 1974, pp. 317–322; W. B. Wolf, "The Impact of Kurt Lewin on Management Thought," *Academy of Management Proceedings*, 1974, pp. 322–325; A. Marrow, *The Practical Theorist: The Life and Work of Kurt Lewin* (New York: Basic Books, 1969).

11. The symposium was published as: O. Klineberg and R. Christie, eds., *Perspectives in Social Psychology* (New York: Holt, Rinehart & Winston, 1965).

12. *Ibid.*, especially S. S. Sargent, "Discussion of Gardner Murphy's Paper."

13. G. Murphy, "The Future of Social Psychology in Historical Perspective," in O. Klineberg and R. Christie, *ibid.*

14. W. J. McGuire, "Discussion of William N. Schoenfeld's Paper," in O. Klineberg and R. Christie, *ibid.*, p. 139.
15. *Ibid.*
16. *Ibid.*, pp. 139–140.
17. *Ibid.*
18. K. Ring, "Experimental Social Psychology: Some Sober Questions About Some Frivolous Values," *Journal of Experimental Social Psychology*, 1967, vol. 3, pp. 112–123. Also pertinent is an article by I. Chein, "Some Sources of Divisiveness Among Psychologists," *American Psychologist*, 1966, vol. 21, pp. 333–342.
19. Ring, as cited.
20. This view is usually associated with the work of George Sarton.
21. Ring, as cited.
22. W. J. McGuire, "Some Impending Reorientations in Social Psychology: Some Thoughts Provoked by Kenneth Ring," *Journal of Experimental Social Psychology*, 1967, vol. 3, pp. 124–139.
23. I. Silverman, "Crisis in Social Psychology: The Relevance of Relevance," *American Psychologist*, 1971, vol. 26, pp. 583–584.
24. *Ibid.*, p. 583. A similar criticism was made by M. Brewster Smith in his review of five volumes of *Advances in Experimental Social Psychology*. In response to the question, *Is experimental social psychology advancing?* he stated: "social psychology still trades more on promise than performance . . . we must conclude that the predominant experimental tradition in the field has contributed rather little for serious export in enlarging and refining our views of social man." See M. B. Smith, "Is Social Psychology Advancing?" *Journal of Experimental Social Psychology*, 1972, vol. 8, pp. 86–96.
25. K. J. Gergen, "Social Psychology as History," *Journal of Personality and Social Psychology*, 1973, vol. 26, pp. 309–320.
26. Also pertinent are: J. R. Kantor, "Psychology: Science or Nonscience?" *Psychological Record*, 1979, vol. 29, pp. 155–163; I. D. London, "Convergent and Divergent Amplification and Its Meaning for Social Science," *Psychological Reports*, 1977, vol. 41, pp. 111–123.
27. See also: P. Brickman and D. T. Campbell, "Hedonic Relativism and Planning the Good Society," in M. H. Appley, ed., *Adaptation-Level Theory* (New York: Academic Press, 1971).
28. Gergen, as cited, p. 316.
29. See, for example, *Personality and Social Psychology Bulletin*, 1976, vol. 2, pp. 384f. Also see B. R. Schlenker, "Social Psychol-

ogy and Science," *Journal of Personality and Social Psychology,* 1974, vol. 29, pp. 1–15.

30. R. L. Rosnow, "Fairs and Psychology's Wares," *American Psychologist,* 1977, vol. 32, pp. 983–985.

31. M. R. Cohen, *Reason and Nature: An Essay on the Meaning of Scientific Method* (New York: Dover, 1959), p. 346.

32. W. J. McGuire, "The Yin and Yang of Progress in Social Psychology: Seven Koan," *Journal of Personality and Social Psychology,* 1973, vol. 26, pp. 446–456.

33. *Ibid.,* p. 449.

34. Silverman, as cited, cautioned: "The experiment should be regarded as the atypical endeavor and experimenters should be required to provide special justification in light of the special problems and limitations inherent in the method." See also the following: U. Neisser, *Cognition and Reality* (San Francisco: W. H. Freeman, 1976), pp. 35–36; J. Deese, "Behavior and Fact," *American Psychologist,* 1969, vol. 24, pp. 515–522; D. Finkleman, "Science and Psychology," *American Journal of Psychology,* 1978, vol. 91, pp. 179–199, especially pp. 188–189; R. Harré and P. F. Secord, *The Explanation of Social Behaviour* (Oxford: Blackwell, 1972); J. Israel and H. Tajfel, *The Context of Social Psychology: A Critical Assessment* (New York: Academic Press, 1972); N. Armistead, *Reconstructing Social Psychology* (Middlesex, England: Penguin, 1974); R. M. Farr, "Experimentation: A Social Psychological Perspective," *British Journal of Social and Clinical Psychology,* 1976, vol. 15, pp. 225–238.

35. For recent developments, see *Handbook of Cross-Cultural Psychology,* edited by Harry C. Triandis et al. (Boston: Allyn and Bacon, 1980). Also pertinent is an article by Claude Faucheux, who points out the deficiency of adequate theoretical foundations for deciding what kind of experimental research is worth doing; see his "Cross-Cultural Research in Experimental Social Psychology," *European Journal of Social Psychology,* 1976, vol. 6, pp. 269–322.

6   Limits of a Paradigm

1. The character is George Passant, and the quote continues: "Now I suspect economics is fundamentally no more difficult than geography. Except that it's about things in motion. If only somebody could invent a dynamic map—" From C. P. Snow's *Strangers and Brothers* (New York: Charles Scribner's Sons, no date), p. 58.

2. Around 1925, Heisenberg realized that the new theory could be proposed only if it were assumed that certain physical microsystems were due to the confluence in quantum mechanics of both a wave theory and particle theory. For discussion, see L. Lanz, "The Uncertainty Principle," Scientia, 1976, vol. 111, pp. 325–332.

3. W. Heisenberg, Physics and Beyond: Encounters and Conversations (New York: Harper & Row, 1971), p. 96.

4. The Newtonian assumptions of the constancy of mass and the proportionality between force and acceleration were now understood to apply only to tangible masses at ordinary velocities. In the realm of small particles moving with velocities comparable to that of light, it was understood that the masses did not remain constant, but varied with velocity. For discussion, see M. R. Cohen, Reason and Nature: An Essay on the Meaning of Scientific Method (New York: Dover, 1978), p. 210.

5. W. Heisenberg, Across the Frontiers (New York: Harper & Row, 1974).

6. Ibid., pp. 43f.

7. Ibid., pp. 185f.

8. See also E. Husserl, The Idea of Phenomenology (The Hague: Nijhoff, 1964), who refers to an "epistemological circle," meaning that the accurate description of a phenomenon is decided by reference to characteristics of descriptive statements rather than by reference to independent criteria. Also see C. Taylor, who writes of an "hermeneutical circle," in "Interpretation and the Sciences of Man," Review of Metaphysics, 1971, vol. 12, pp. 5–52. Both pertain to the notion of a stylized or restricted frame of reference.

9. For discussions, see: A. R. Buss, "On the Relationship Between Causes and Reasons," Journal of Personality and Social Psychology, 1979, vol. 37, pp. 1458–1461; R. E. Lana, "Attribution Theory and the Dialectic in Social Psychology," Temple University, unpublished manuscript, 1980.

10. In drawing this distinction, I refer to Eugene Rosa's illuminating article "Sociobiology, Biosociology, or Vulgar Biologizing," Sociological Symposium, 1979, summer issue, no. 27, pp. 26–50.

11. E. O. Wilson, Sociobiology: The New Synthesis (Cambridge, Mass.: Belknap/Harvard University Press, 1975).

12. D. P. Barash, Sociobiology and Behavior (New York: Elsevier, 1977).

13. Gustave LeBon, the early social psychologist, was also greatly in-

fluenced by the evolutionary concept. In his *Psychology of the Evolution of Peoples*, he attempted to show how institutions, languages, beliefs, etc., were transformed by a process of incessant evolution into higher forms. For discussion, see *Gustave LeBon: The Man and His Works*, translated by A. Widener (Indianapolis: Liberty Press, 1979).

14. The term was presumably coined in the eighteenth century by Johann Gottfried von Herder, the great German philosopher and poet. It also appears in Goethe's *Faust* (*"geist der zeiten"*) and was introduced into English by Matthew Arnold, the poet and literary critic, in 1893 in his book *Literature and Dogma*, where it was used to denote a general "temper" or "feeling" characteristic of a particular period of time.

15. See also discussion in E. G. Boring, *A History of Experimental Psychology* (New York: Appleton-Century-Crofts, 1957).

16. In its original usage, a cohort meant a company of warriors—a cohort was one of ten divisions in an ancient Roman legion. For sociological introduction, see N. B. Ryder, "The Cohort as a Concept in the Study of Social Change," *American Sociological Review*, 1965, vol. 30, pp. 843–861. Ryder defines cohort as the aggregate of individuals, within some population, who experienced the same events in the same time frame.

17. See H. E. Jones and H. S. Conrad, "The Growth and Decline of Intelligence: The Study of a Homogeneous Group Between the Age of 10 to 60," *Genetic Psychology Monographs*, 1933, vol. 13, pp. 223–298.

18. R. D. Tuddenham, "Soldier Intelligence in World Wars I and II," *American Psychologist*, 1948, vol. 3, pp. 149–159.

19. See, for example, discussion by K. F. Riegel, "Influence of Economic and Political Ideologies on the Development of Developmental Psychology," *Psychological Bulletin*, 1972, vol. 78, pp. 129–141.

20. *Ibid.*, p. 139. For alternative research designs, see K. W. Schaie, "A General Model for the Study of Developmental Problems," *Psychological Bulletin*, 1965, vol. 64, pp. 92–108; P. B. Baltes, "Longitudinal and Cross-Sectional Sequences in the Study of Age and Generation Effects," *Human Development*, 1968, vol. 11, pp. 145–171.

21. L. Festinger, *A Theory of Cognitive Dissonance* (Stanford, Cal.: Stanford University Press, 1962).

22. W. B. Cannon, *The Wisdom of the Body*, revised edition (New York: Norton, 1932).

23. W. Köhler, The Place of Value in a World of Facts (New York: Liveright, 1938).

24. For the latest version, see R. A. Wicklund and J. W. Brehm, Perspectives on Cognitive Dissonance (Hillside, N.J.: Erlbaum, 1976). For discussion of the evolution of Festinger's theory, see A. G. Greenwald and D. L. Ronis, "Twenty Years of Cognitive Dissonance: Case Study of the Evolution of a Theory," Psychological Review, 1978, vol. 85, pp. 53–59.

25. See, for example, R. H. Fazio, M. P. Zanna, and J. Cooper, "Dissonance and Self-Perception: An Integrative View of Each Theory's Proper Domain of Application," Journal of Experimental Social Psychology, 1977, vol. 13, pp. 464–479.

26. For a recent experimental study that sought to break out of this mold by examining the use of historical knowledge to test attribution hypotheses, see M. Snyder and N. Cantor, "Testing Hypotheses About Other People: The Use of Historical Knowledge," Journal of Experimental Social Psychology, 1979, vol. 15, pp. 330–342.

27. See Allport's discussions of prejudice in G. W. Allport, The Person in Psychology: Selected Essays (Boston: Beacon Press, 1968) and G. W. Allport, The Nature of Prejudice (New York: Doubleday/Anchor, 1954).

28. F. A. Blanchard, L. Adelman, and S. W. Cook, "Effect of Group Success and Failure Upon Interpersonal Attraction in Cooperating Interracial Groups," Journal of Personality and Social Psychology, 1975, vol. 31, pp. 1020–1030; S. W. Cook (with the collaboration of L. S. Wrightsman, S. Wrightsman, and J. Nottingham), "The Effect of Unintended Interracial Contact Upon Racial Interaction and Attitude Change," final report to U.S. Dept. of Health, Education and Welfare (Project 5-1320), August 1971; R. H. Weigel and S. W. Cook, "Participation in Decision-Making: A Determinant of Interpersonal Attraction in Cooperating Interracial Groups," International Journal of Group Tensions, 1975, vol. 5, pp. 179–195.

29. L. A. Foley, "Personality and Situational Influences on Changes in Prejudice: A Replication of Cook's Railroad Game in a Prison Setting," Journal of Personality and Social Psychology, 1976, vol. 34, pp. 846–856; M. Deutsch and M. E. Collins, Interracial Housing: A Psychological Evaluation of a Social Experiment (Minneapolis: University of Minnesota Press, 1951); E. Grier and G. Grier, Privately Developed Interracial Housing (Berkeley: University of California Press, 1960).

30. G. L. Clore, R. M. Bray, S. M. Itkin, and P. Murphy, "Interracial Attitudes and Behavior at a Summer Camp," *Journal of Personality and Social Psychology,* 1978, vol. 36, pp. 107–116.
31. W. J. McGuire, "The Yin and Yang of Progress in Social Psychology: Seven Koan," *Journal of Personality and Social Psychology,* 1973, vol. 26, pp. 446–456.
32. D. A. Taylor, *Root and Branch: Toward the Elimination of Prejudice and Racism,* in preparation. See also discussion by Y. Amir, Contact Hypothesis in Ethnic Relations," *Psychological Bulletin,* 1969, vol. 71, pp. 319–342.
33. R. L. Rosnow, "The Prophetic Vision of Giambattista Vico: Implications for the State of Social Psychological Theory," *Journal of Personality and Social Psychology,* 1978, vol. 36, pp. 1322–1331, especially p. 1323.
34. See discussion by C. W. Mills, "Situated Actions and the Vocabularies of Motive," *American Sociological Review,* 1940, vol. 5, pp. 904–913.
35. E. E. Sampson, "Psychology and the American Ideal," *Journal of Personality and Social Psychology,* 1977, vol. 35, pp. 767–782.
36. William Safire, the political writer, gives a good example of this point. He mentions that, at a Peking banquet in 1972, Premier Zhou Enlai placed a morsel of food from his plate on the plate of Richard Nixon. Nixon responded correctly by nodding his thanks. But in January 1980, when Defense Secretary Harold Brown found himself in a similar situation during his trip to China, he was unaware of the cultural symbolism and responded exactly the wrong way—by plunking a morsel of his own back on the plate of his Chinese host. Brown was responding according to the Western notion of reciprocity, but for the Chinese host the morsel placed on a guest's plate was an act complete in itself. See W. Safire, "The Chinese Morsel," *The New York Times,* January 21, 1980, Op-Ed page.
37. Discussion by Cohen, as cited.

7 Reconstruction of Social Psychology

1. M. R. Cohen, *Reason and Nature: An Essay on the Meaning of Scientific Method* (New York: Dover, 1978), p. 352.
2. A pointer reading is any relatively undisputed confirmatory measure. See J. C. Pepper, *World Hypotheses: A Study in Evidence* (Berkeley: University of California Press, 1970), pp. 52f. This use

of experiments to *qualify* a negative assertion is, of course, a different idea than Popper's emphasis on falsification as a critical criterion and, I believe, it may be closer to the Duhem-Quine idea in the sense that pointer readings would imply the impossibility of a crucial falsifying experiment in social psychology. See discussions by K. R. Popper, *The Logic of Scientific Discovery* (New York: Harper & Row, 1965); P. Duhem, *The Aim and Structure of Physical Theory* (Princeton, N.J.: Princeton University Press, 1954). For general discussion of this issue, see W. B. Weimer, *Notes on the Methodology of Scientific Research* (Hillsdale, N.J.: Erlbaum, 1979).

3. See discussion by E. G. Boring, "Perspective: Artifact and Control," in R. Rosenthal and R. L. Rosnow, eds., *Artifact in Behavioral Research* (New York: Academic Press, 1969).

4. R. L. Solomon, "An Extension of Control Group Design," *Psychological Bulletin*, 1949, vol. 46, pp. 137–150.

5. D. T. Campbell and J. C. Stanley, *Experimental and Quasi-Experimental Designs for Research* (Chicago, Illinois: Rand McNally, 1966).

6. R. E. Lana, "Pretest Sensitization," in R. Rosenthal and R. L. Rosnow, eds., *Artifact in Behavioral Research* (New York: Academic Press, 1969).

7. R. L. Rosnow and J. M. Suls, "Reactive Effects of Pretesting in Attitude Research," *Journal of Personality and Social Psychology*, 1970, vol. 15, pp. 338–343.

8. See also K. J. Gergen, "Experimentation in Social Psychology: A Reappraisal," *European Journal of Social Psychology*, 1978, vol. 8, pp. 507–527.

9. Drawn from S. D. Ross, *Moral Decision: An Introduction to Ethics* (San Francisco: Freeman, Cooper, 1972), p. 46—but used in a different connection.

10. See D. T. Campbell, "Reforms as Experiments," *American Psychologist*, 1969, vol. 24, pp. 409–429.

11. For pertinent discussions, see: I. L. Horowitz, "Methods and Strategies in Evaluating Equity Research," *Social Indicators Research*, 1979, vol. 6, pp. 1–22; H. W. Riecken, "Social Experimentation," *Society*, July/August 1975, pp. 34–41.

12. For discussion of theoretical differences, see E. R. Hilgard, *Theories of Learning* (New York: Appleton-Century-Crofts, 1956).

13. M. B. Jones and R. S. Fennell, III, "Runway Performance in Two Strains of Rats," *Quarterly Journal of the Florida Academy of Sciences*, 1965, vol. 28, pp. 289–296.

14. The fundamental postulate of mechanism is that there is an ultimate structure of things for the physicist to discover, but in social psychology it is also necessary, as Cohen has stated, to "draw a distinction between the microscopic view of human purpose, between the little drops of human volition, and the general social streams which result from them." See Cohen as cited, p. 342.

15. See discussion by M. Granovetter, "The Idea of 'Advancement' in Theories of Social Evolution and Development," *American Journal of Sociology*, 1979, vol. 85, pp. 489–515.

16. For general discussions of these three models, see R. A. Nisbet, *Social Change and History: Aspects of the Western Theory of Development* (New York: Oxford University Press, 1969); and R. P. Appelbaum, *Theories of Social Change* (Chicago, Markham, 1970). It may be true, as in physics, that the use of more than one system may be a permanent necessity for full coordination of our facts. See discussion by R. H. Thouless, "The Place of Theory in Experimental Psychology," *British Journal of Psychology*, 1950, vol. 41, especially p. 23, in which this notion is developed specifically in regard to theories such as the Freudian and Gestalt formulations.

17. Quoted from Applebaum, as cited, p. 19.

18. For discussion of kinship theory, see R. L. Trivers and H. Hare, "Haploidiploidy and the Evolution of the Social Insects," *Science*, 1976, vol. 191, pp. 249–263. Also see S. R. Witkowski, "Kinship," *American Behavioral Scientist*, 1977, vol. 20, pp. 657–668.

19. See critique by R. Hofstadter, *Social Darwinism in American Thought* (Boston: Beacon Press, 1955).

20. For arguments for-and-against, see: M. Shapiro, *The Sociobiology of Homo Sapiens* (Kansas City, Mo.: Pinecrest Fund, 1978); E. O. Wilson, *On Human Nature* (Cambridge, Mass.: Harvard University Press, 1978); M. S. Gregory, A. Silvers, and D. Sutch, eds., *Sociobiology and Human Nature* (San Francisco: Jossey-Bass, 1978). Other pertinent work is by J. E. Pfeiffer, *The Emergence of Society: A Prehistory of the Establishment* (New York: McGraw-Hill, 1977); J. Friedman and M. J. Rowland, eds., *The Evolution of Social Systems* (Pittsburgh, Pa.: University of Pittsburgh Press, 1978); M. J. Harner, "Population Pressures and the Social Evolution of Agriculturists," *Southwestern Journal of Anthropology*, 1970, vol. 26, pp. 67–86; R. J. Carneiro, "A Theory of the Origin of the State," *Science*, 1970, vol. 169, pp. 733–738.

21. J. Piaget, *The Origins of Intelligence in Children* (New York: Nor-

ton, 1952); J. Piaget, *Structuralism* (New York: Basic Books, 1970).

22. C. Martindale, "The Evolution of English Poetry," *Poetics*, 1978, vol. 7, pp. 231–248.

23. For a particularly bold theory on the evolution of human consciousness, see J. Jaynes, *The Origin of Consciousness in the Breakdown of the Bicameral Mind* (Boston: Houghton Mifflin, 1977).

24. G. Vico, *Principles of New Science of Giambattista Vico Concerning the Nature of the Nations*, translated and edited by T. G. Bergin and M. H. Fisch (Ithaca, N.Y.: Cornell University Press, 1975). For discussion of relevance to social theory, see the following: I. Berlin, *Vico and Herder: Two Studies in the History of Ideas* (New York: Vintage Books, 1976); R. L. Rosnow, "The Prophetic Vision of Giambattista Vico: Implications for the State of Social Psychological Theory," *Journal of Personality and Social Psychology*, 1978, vol. 36, pp. 1322–1331;) R. E. Lana, "Giambattista Vico and the History of Social Psychology," *Journal for the Theory of Social Behaviour*, 1980, vol. 9, pp. 251–263.

25. O. Spengler, "The Life Cycle of Cultures," in A. Etzioni and E. Etzioni, eds., *Social Change* (New York: Basic Books, 1964) P. A. Sorokin, "A Survey of the Cyclical Conceptions of Social and Historical Processes," *Social Forces*, 1927, vol. 6, pp. 28–40; F. S. Chapin, "A Theory of Synchronous Culture Cycles," *Journal of Social Forces*, 1925; vol. 3, pp. 596–604; M. Weber, *The Theory of Social and Economic Organizations* (New York: Free Press, 1964).

26. Rosnow, as cited. LeBon also alluded to cycle synchronies when he wrote: "regressive evolution being much faster than ascendant evolution, people take centuries to acquire a certain mental structure and sometimes lose it very fast." See *Gustave LeBon: The Man and His Works*, translated by A. Widener (Indianapolis: Liberty Press, 1979), p. 275.

27. W. J. McGuire, "Historical Comparisons: Testing Psychological Hypotheses With Cross-Era Data," *International Journal of Psychology*, 1976, vol. 11, pp. 161–183.

28. For discussion, see R. L. Rosnow and G. A. Fine, *Rumor and Gossip: The Social Psychology of Hearsay* (New York: Elsevier, 1976); R. L. Rosnow, "Psychology of Rumor Reconsidered," *Psychological Bulletin*, 1980, vol. 87, pp. 578–591.

29. C. G. Jung, *Flying Saucers: A Modern Myth of Things Seen in the Skies*, reprinted in *The Collected Works of C. G. Jung*, vol. 10 (New York: Bollingen Series XX/Pantheon Books, 1964).

30. E. R. Dewey, *Cycles: Selected Writings* (Pittsburgh, Pa.: Foundation for the Study of Cycles, 1970).
31. For Frankfurt School, see work of J. Habermas, *Knowledge and Human Interests* (Boston: Beacon Press, 1971); M. Horkheimer, *Critical Theory* (New York: Seabury, 1973); T. W. Adorno et al., eds. *The Positivist Dispute in German Sociology* (New York: Harper & Row, 1976).
32. G.W.F. Hegel, *On Art, Religion, Philosophy: Introductory Lectures to the Realm of Absolute Spirit*, edited by J. G. Gray (New York: Harper Torchbooks, 1970), p. 259.
33. See discussion by G. Allan, "Sartre's Constriction of the Marxist Dialectic," *Review of Metaphysics*, 1979, vol. 33, pp. 87–108.
34. N. J. Smelser, "Stability, Instability, and the Analysis of Political Corruption," in B. Barber and A. Inkeles, eds., *Stability and Social Change* (Boston: Little, Brown, 1971), quoted from p. 7.
35. H. C. Werner and B. Kaplan, *Symbol Formation: An Organismic-Developmental Approach to Language and the Expression of Thought* (New York: Wiley, 1963).
36. K. F. Riegel, "Influence of Economic and Political Ideologies on the Development of Developmental Psychology," *Psychological Bulletin*, 1972, vol. 78, pp. 129–141; K. F. Riegel, "The Dialectics of Human Development," *American Psychologist*, 1976, vol. 31, pp. 689–700.
37. R. E. Lana, "Attribution Theory and the Dialectic in Social Psychology," Temple University, unpublished manuscript, 1980.
38. See the following for work that is pertinent: G. J. Mellenbergh, "The Replicability of Measures," *Psychological Bulletin*, 1977, vol. 84, pp. 378–384; R. Rosenthal, "Combining Results of Independent Studies," *Psychological Bulletin*, 1978, vol. 85, pp. 185–193; For theoretical application to social psychology, see also Rosnow, "The Prophetic Vision of Giambattista Vico," as cited.
39. H. M. Cooper, "Statistically Combining Independent Studies: A Meta-Analysis of Sex Differences in Conformity Research," *Journal of Personality and Social Psychology*, 1979, vol. 37, pp. 131–146.
40. A. H. Eagly, "Sex Differences in Influenceability," *Psychological Bulletin*, 1978, vol. 85, pp. 86–116.
41. M. W. Riley and E. E. Nelson, "Research on Stability and Change in Social Systems," in B. Barber and A. Inkeles, eds., *Stability and Social Change* (Boston: Little, Brown, 1971), p. 411.
42. It is also important to draw a distinction as to the exact level of human activity that is of concern. Thus, Albert Pepitone has

recently pointed out how our theoretical unit of analysis is often misplaced in social psychology. Our research methodology is usually on an intraindividual level, he notes, but much of the social behavior that we attempt to explain is interindividual and normative, in being more characteristic of groups, classes, roles and other sociocultural systems. A similar point was made by Willard W. Hartup, who argued that observational studies in developmental-social psychology have focused almost exclusively on peer-group behavior, but extrapolations are casually made to cross-age interactions. See A. Pepitone, "Toward a Normative and Comparative Biocultural Social Psychology," *Journal of Personality and Social Psychology,* 1976, vol. 4, pp. 641–653; W. W. Hartup, "Cross-Age Versus Same-Age Peer Interaction: Ethological and Cross-Cultural Perspectives," in V. Allen, ed., *Children as Teachers: Theory and Research on Tutoring* (New York: Academic Press, 1976).

43. McGuire, as cited.
44. D. K. Simonton, "Cross-Sectional Time-Series Experiments: Some Suggested Statistical Analyses," *Psychological Bulletin,* 1977, vol. 84, pp. 489–502.
45. McGuire, as cited, for discussion.
46. D. J. Simonton, "The Sociopolitical Context of Philosophical Beliefs: A Transhistorical Causal Analysis," *Social Forces,* 1976, vol. 54, pp. 513–523.
47. D. K. Simonton, "Land Battles, Generals, and Armies: Individual and Situational Determinants of Victory and Casualties," *Journal of Personality and Social Psychology,* 1980, vol. 38, pp. 110–119.
48. See, for example, the following: R. Rosenthal, *Experimenter Effects in Behavioral Research: Enlarged Edition* (New York: Irvington Publishers, Halsted Press Division of Wiley, 1976); R. Rosenthal and R. L Rosnow, *The Volunteer Subject* (New York: Wiley-Interscience, 1975); R. L. Rosnow and D. J. Davis, "Demand Characteristics and the Psychological Experiment," *Et Cetera: A Review of General Semantics,* 1977, vol. 34, pp. 301–313.
49. See discussion by L. Freese and M. Rokeach, "On the Use of Alternative Interpretations in Contemporary Social Psychology," *Social Psychology Quarterly,* 1979, vol. 42, pp. 195–201.
50. See discussion of triangulation method in E. J. Webb, D. T. Campbell, R. D. Schwartz, and L. Sechrest, *Unobtrusive Measures: Nonreactive Research in the Social Sciences* (Chicago: Rand McNally, 1966).
51. Particularly noteworthy is the research by Joseph V. Brady and

his associates. See J. V. Brady, G. Bigelow, H. Emurian, and D. M. Williams, "Design of a Programmed Environment for the Experimental Analysis of Social Behavior," in D. H. Carson, ed., *Man-Environment Interactions: Evaluations and Applications* (Milwaukee, Wis.: Environmental Design Research Associates, 1974), pp. 187–208; J. V. Brady and H. H. Emurian, "Behavior Analysis of Motivational and Emotional Interactions in a Programmed Environment," *Nebraska Symposium on Motivation*, 1978. By studying volunteer subjects in a social ecology that is continuously measured, these researchers have shown how it is possible to generate pointer readings of changeable motivational and emotional states within a given time frame. Of course, it is precisely the unpredictable changes in sociocultural trends that would probably account for the most difficulties in forecasting beyond this situation.

52. See discussion by U. G. Foa, "Three Kinds of Behavioral Change," *Psychological Bulletin*, 1968, vol. 70, pp. 460–473.

53. Egon Brunswik, who introduced the notion of a representative experimental design, argued that the nomothetic behaviorism of Hull and Tolman had overexpanded physicalism beyond its necessary observational and procedural core. Seldom did experimenters sample from among stimuli and situations as they did from among subject populations, Brunswik asserted. Yet, simply by avoiding a double standard (in scrutinizing subject generality while ignoring the representativeness of other significant elements of the experimental situation) we may also begin to solidify the area of application of the experimental method within obvious limitations. See E. Brunswik, "Representative Design and Probabilistic Theory in a Functional Psychology," *Psychological Review*, 1955, vol. 62, pp. 193–217. See also discussions by K. R. Hammond, "Subject and Object Sampling—A Note," *Psychological Bulletin*, 1948, vol. 45, pp. 530–533; K. R. Hammond, "Relativity and Representativeness," *Philosophy of Science*, 1951, vol. 18, pp 201–211; K. R. Hammond, "Representative Vs. Systematic Design in Clinical Psychology," *Psychological Bulletin*, 1954, vol. 51, pp. 150–159.

54. See, for example, discussions by J. A. Hagenaars and N. P. Cobben, "Age, Cohort, and Period: A General Model for the Analysis of Social Change," *Netherlands Journal of Sociology*, 1978, vol. 14, pp. 59–91; P. B. Baltes, H. W. Reese, and L. P. Lipsitt, "Life-Span Developmental Psychology," *Annual Review of Psychology*, 1980, vol. 31, pp. 65–110; T. D. Cook and D. T. Campbell,

Quasi-Experimentation: Design and Analysis Issues for Field Settings (Chicago: Rand McNally, 1979); J. W. Tukey, *Exploratory Data Analysis* (Reading, Mass.: Addison-Wesley, 1977); N. B. Tuma, M. T. Hannan, and L. P. Groeneveld, "Dynamic Analysis of Event Histories," *American Journal of Sociology*, 1979, vol. 84, pp. 820–854; J. M. Gottman, "Detecting Cyclicity in Social Interaction," *Psychological Bulletin*, 1979, vol. 86, pp. 338–348; D. A. Kenny, *Correlation and Causality* (New York: Wiley-Interscience, 1979).

55. See, for example, discussions by J. P. Roos, "From Oddball Research to the Study of Real Life: The Use of Qualitative Methods in Social Science," *Acta Sociologica*, 1979, vol. 22, pp. 63–74; G. Holton, "On the Role of Themata in Scientific Thought," *Science*, 1975, vol. 188, pp. 328–334.

56. For review and partial bibliography, see D. H. Zimmerman, "Ethnomethodology," *American Sociologist*, 1978, vol. 13, pp. 6–15.

57. I agree with Paul E. Meehl when he wrote: "It is vulgar positivism (still held by many psychologists) to insist that any respectable empirical theory must be testable if testable means *definitively testable right now.*" See P. E. Meehl, "Theoretical Risks and Tabular Asterisks: Sir Karl, Sir Ronald, and the Slow Progress of Soft Psychology," *Journal of Consulting and Clinical Psychology*, 1978, vol. 46, pp. 806–834, quoted from p. 830.

8   Review and Conclusions

1. A. Kaplan, *The Conduct of Inquiry: Methodology for Behavioral Science* (Scranton, Pa.: Chandler, 1964), pp. 28–29.

2. Einstein mentions that had Leibniz's justified doubts won out at the time, it hardly would have been beneficial to physics, for the empirical and theoretical foundations necessary to pursue this vision were not available in the seventeenth century. See A. Einstein, "On the Generalized Theory," *Scientific American*, 1950, vol. 209, pp. 3–7.

3. Social psychology might have begun as a relativistic, but still an essentially deterministic, dynamic system—perhaps more on the order of Galilean cosmology. The Indians have an ancient cyclical idea of time as a kind of cosmic mechanism, the notion that there is an eternal recurrence and that time repeats the same pattern over and over again. This view of change as something natural and primary also goes back to the ancient Greeks, who believed that there is an historical pattern that repeats itself

continuously. Indeed it is this correspondence between Greek philosophy, in particular Platonic philosophy, and the Christian religion that seems a key integrative element in the development of mystical religion in the West. See discussion on this point by W. H. Capps and W. M. Wright, *Silent Fire: An Invitation to Western Mysticism* (Princeton, N.J.: Princeton University Press, 1959).

4. *Ecclesiastes* I: 2–11.

5. See discussions by R. A. Nisbet, *Social Change and History: Aspects of the Western Theory of Development* (New York: Oxford University Press, 1969); W. F. Overton, "The Active Organism in Structuralism," *Human Development*, 1976, vol. 19, pp. 71–86; J. R. Royce, H. Coward, E. Egan, F. Kessel, and L. Mos, "Psychological Epistemology: A Critical Review of the Empirical Literature and the Theoretical Issues," *Genetic Psychology Monographs*, 1978, vol. 97, pp. 265–353.

6. For discussion, see W. D. Hackmann, "The Relationship Between Concept and Instrument Design in Eighteenth-Century Experimental Science," *Annals of Science*, 1979, vol. 36, pp. 205–224, especially pp. 220f.

7. H. P. Adams, *The Life and Writings of Giambattista Vico,* (London: George Allen & Unwin, 1935), p. 172.

8. Some experimentalists, such as William McGuire and Robert Wyer, have tried to deal with exactly this problem of making allowance for probabilistic conclusions in formal logic. See, for example, R. S. Wyer, Jr., "Effects of Previously Formed Beliefs on Syllogistic Inference Processes," *Journal of Personality and Social Psychology*, 1976, vol. 33, pp. 307–316.

9. Discussion by I. I. Mitroff and R. H. Kilmann, *Methodological Approaches to Social Science* (San Francisco: Jossey-Bass, 1978).

10. Joseph Margolis writes: "A modern physician, aware of an enormous range of possible error and the like, may be less certain with respect to the same matter than the naive primitive, to whom relevant doubts will not even have occurred or been weighed or set aside as unlikely; yet, without a doubt, the physician may be said, with more justice or at least equal justice, to know about the treatment of the disorder in question. Also, the very certainty of the primitive may, under the circumstances, count to some extent against his having knowledge; or, if it is allowed because relativized to his cultural setting, assessing the relative certainty of the modern physician may, at an even later stage of science, be similarly affected." See J. Margolis, *Knowl-*

edge and Existence: An Introduction to Philosophical Problems (New York: Oxford University Press, 1973), p. 33.

11. W. J. McGuire, "The Nature of Attitudes and Opinions," in G. Lindzey and E. Aronson, eds., The Handbook of Social Psychology, second edition (Reading, Mass.: Addison-Wesley, 1969).

12. I. Berlin, The Hedgehog and the Fox: An Essay on Tolstoy's View of History (New York: Simon & Schuster, 1953).

Index